# 'The Witch Biker's Ride through the Balance Sheet'

## By

## Richard France MBA, FCA

ISBN-13: 978-1490998800

ISBN-10: 1490998802

# Table of Contents

# Introduction

This book has been written to help students of business or finance who are meeting accounting and finance for the first time at a Further or Higher Education level. It is intended to engage the student by using relevant examples and humour with a few outrageous, although (hopefully) inoffensive, situations. The book is an ongoing fictional story about a developing business with the owner, Jack Whackhead, who starts a clothing company and seeking and getting regular advice from his accountant, Ashna Mukherjee.

The target audience is any student encountering finance and accounting for the first time although principally it is aimed at the following groups:

- University or College First Year Business Studies Students
- University or College First Year Accounting & Finance Students
- HND & HNC students
- Students undertaking a Business or Combined Business Foundation degree
- Entrepreneurs or budding entrepreneurs who have ideas of running their own business

This book includes many worked examples and is primarily intended as a teaching aid. Further academic explanation of some topic areas is referenced at the ends of the chapters and lies in the Appendices so as not to disturb the flow unduly. It has been written in a style to engage the student at a price that hopefully students should afford!

# ACKNOWLEDGEMENTS

In writing this book, I would like to place on record my thanks to the thousands (literally) of students that have steered me towards a way of making the topics more understandable and relevant by showing their feelings through REM (Rapid Eye Movement) sleep behaviour.

My particular thanks to Asha Lad, MMU Accounting and Finance Undergraduate student, who reviewed this book from a student's perspective.

All characters in this publication are entirely fictitious and any resemblance to real persons, living or dead, is purely coincidental.

# 1. Scenario Overview

Jack Whackhead was walking along a dark and dusty road in the northern English town of Crewe one wet, windy Thursday evening at 8.30pm having just finished work. He was a young man of 24 and felt on this occasion to be about 70 as he was extremely tired having just finished working for his lunatic boss, Ben Crustybonce, who seemed to want to slowly drain the energy out of him through giving him the most mind-numbing, spirit-crushing work imaginable. His job was to remove the excess bits from the edges of pottery that had been fired in a kiln. It was, he believed, called 'fettling'. He had to do this with a tool that was clearly crafted in the dark ages and his hands got regularly burnt from handling the very hot items as there was never time to wait for them to cool. Today he wanted to strangle Mr Crustybonce with one of his own ties which he always wore to give him some feeling of authority even though his tie never matched anything he was wearing but regularly matched his lunch.

As he walked home to his flat, he wondered what he would be doing in 5 years' time as the thought of carrying on with this was enough to send him to the funny farm. He had a small flat in which his sometime girlfriend, Ziggy Pretzel, refused to stay as she thought it was too small and in a horrible area of the town. It was somewhat a relief she felt this way as this relationship had probably run its course. The flat was also permanently untidy as his mental state prevented him from retrieving a single item from the floor as it would be covering some unseemly mess underneath. All in all he was at his wit's end when suddenly there was a flash of lightning and in front of him was a clothing shop with all the cool items that he had wanted to buy when at University but could not afford. Like George Best, much of his money had gone on girls and alcohol and the rest he had wasted so he never had any decent clothing. He stared at the window and, as if by some power beyond his clanking brain, the germ of an idea was formed in his mind. He would start trading in clothing! He had always had a passion for it and he surely could not earn less than he currently did fettling the pottery. Why not? He was young, not too bad looking although a bit of a meathead and a big guy who could take care of himself.

Big problem. He only had £500 in his bank account and that would not get him very far so he resolved to use some of it to test his abilities to trade at a profit. He knew that a profit was made when you sell at a price that was higher than your costs so he resolved to give it a go. He already had an Ebay account so he turned it into a sales account and decided he would start gently by buying a few choice items from a local clothing wholesaler (someone who buys in bulk and sells to other businesses in small quantities). The owner's name was Crosby Blob and he went to see him the next day. They agreed that Jack would purchase 6 men's jumpers for £10 each and Crosby said he could probably sell them for £15 each (a £5 or 50% mark-up on cost) giving him a profit of £5 per sweater or £5 x 6 = £30 if he sold all of them. Jack soon realised that if he spent 6 x £10 = £60 he would need to get back at least £60 so as not to be out of pocket. If he sold them at £15 that would mean he would need to sell 4 (4 x £15 = £60) to get his money back so his profit would only come when he sold at least 5.

Sure enough he got started and placed them on Ebay at the 'buy it now' price of £15 each. Within a week he had sold all of them and checked how much his bank had altered and had a big disappointment. Instead of it going up by £30 it had only increased by £20!

# 2.    The Income Statement

He decided that he would need an accountant to explain a few things to him and through a series of contacts from old college friends he came across Ashna Mukherjee, a young qualified accountant who specialised in helping small businesses to grow. She was very pleasant and never stopped smiling and Jack could not decide if it was that she found his name, Jack Whackhead, funny or because she felt sorry for his complete lack of financial understanding. He wondered if she used teeth whitening or maybe she just had a good diet because her pearly whites were as bright as any he had seen. Anyway, she agreed to take him on as a client and she would not charge him until he was making a reasonable profit but he would have to fit his time around her spare time. He realised this was an incredibly generous offer and straightaway he felt comfortable with her as she explained why his bank account had not increased as he had expected.

She explained the following to him about the principal financial statements of a company.

Firstly, there are three main accounting statements for a trading company. These are called the Income Statement (Profit & Loss account), the Balance Sheet, (Statement of Financial Position - SOFP) and the Statement of Cash Flows. The statement of cash flows tends to be only produced for larger companies and she said she would explain that later in Jack's trading life but he really needed to know about the other two very quickly if he was to make a success of his venture as the principle 'stakeholder'. Additionally there were the budgets for the next year to be considered and their likely effect on the cash position at the bank.

Ashna drew him the following picture to highlight the main statements.

# *Main Statements*

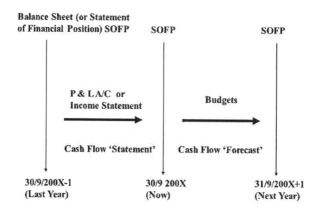

She then asked him if he understood what a stakeholder was and he could not help himself. "I guess it is the person who looks after the big slab of meat before it goes under the grill." He followed this with a raucous laugh and realised immediately that acting the fool was not his most endearing quality at this specific moment in time. She quickly brought him down to size. "I think you know a little more than that. In any case, 'stake' is spelt differently to the 'steak' to which you refer. A stakeholder is anyone with an interest in the business and all the stakeholders could have some interest in the accounts of the business. Give me an example of a stakeholder, Jack."

"Well, there's me and there's ...... me and ...... there's me. Oh and yes maybe the tax authorities."

"Good Jack, now you're thinking" cut in Ashna. "There are many stakeholders to a business and the 'Primary' stakeholders are key stakeholders and usually have some contractual relationship such as the owner like yourself, the bank, the suppliers, customers or employees. The 'Secondary' stakeholders might be such as any local residents near your operation who might be affected by your work such as noise or traffic. Alternatively, an example might be an environmental protection organisation that is interested in your waste and recycling. All of these might have an interest and the accounts could supply them with useful information; that is if they are published or you give them a copy."

"I would not do that. I am not that stupid."

"You might have no choice as the bank may not lend you money without seeing the accounts and anyway if you became a Limited Company the accounts are published anyway. We shall come on to that later though."

"Oh", shrugged Jack. "I guess I have no choice then."

"Maybe, maybe not, but the point is there are other stakeholders besides you and you have a need to satisfy them in differing capacities. Anyway, let's look at the first accounting statement. The Income Statement or Profit & Loss Account (as it is also known) summarises all the sales made in a period and from that figure all of the costs are deducted in making those sales plus any other costs of running the business.

It will be shown as an example as follows:

Income Statement for Jack Whackhead Clothing for the year ended 30<sup>th</sup> June 2014

| | |
|---|---|
| Sales | £10,000 |
| Less Costs | 9,000 |
| Profit | £1,000 |

The sales (also known as revenue, income or turnover) is all the work done for the customers whether as a service (like an accountant) or in supplying products like Jack. The customers would be sent an Invoice which is the source document for the entry into the books of account to record a sale. Note that a company with a turnover of currently greater than £79,000 (UK) would need to be registered for Value Added Tax (sales tax), in which case you would send an invoice for £150 plus 20% vat = £180. The £30 tax would be then passed on to the HMRC. (Taxation Notes Appendices Part 1/9)

The costs need to be broken down into two main areas called Cost of Sales and Expenses (or Overheads) so the Income statement would now be shown as follows:

| Sales | £10,000 |
|---|---|
| Less Cost of Sales | £4,000 |
| Gross Profit | £6,000 |
| Less Overheads | 5,000 |
| Profit | £1,000 |

The total costs are still £9,000 but taken off in two bites. The cost of sales would be the direct or basic costs of the products bought. In your case Jack, the cost of the clothing from the wholesaler and the overheads would then be all the rest of the costs such as motor expenses, heating, electricity etc."

"That still does not explain why I have less in the bank than I planned" exclaimed Jack between coughs as he was gasping for a cigarette and for some strange reason he coughed less when he smoked than when he gave up for a while.

"OK, well let's look at the costs then. You say you purchased the jumpers for £10 each. That's £60. Did you pay cash? By that I mean was it immediate payment or did mean old Crosby give you any credit?"

"Yes, I paid straight away when I picked up the jumpers."

"Did you get £15 for each of them through Ebay and did you sell them all?"

"Yes" said Jack raising his eyes to the ceiling.

"Do Ebay charge you for their services and what about packaging and postage to the customers?"

At times finance was as unclear as a leather lantern but a glimmer of light was beginning to appear in Jack's brain as he realised there were other costs. "Aha, I paid about £1.50 each for the postage and Ebay costs were about £12 in total."

In that case your Income Statement for the period would look like this:

| Sales | (6 × £15) | £90 |
|---|---|---|
| Less Cost of Sales | (6 × £10) | 60 |
| Gross Profit | | 30 |
| Less Overheads | | |
| Postage (6 × £1.50) | 9 | |
| Ebay Costs | 12 | 21 |
| Profit | | £9 |

So, provided you paid immediately for your supplies and all the customers paid you straightaway you should have £9 extra in the bank at the end.

"Eureka". Now Jack was beginning to see her worth as it became clear to him that there was much he needed to grasp if he was to make his million before he reached 30. He also realised that the sales or cost of sales figures did not change if either were done on credit as it was about the invoices in and out that determined the profit and not the cash although in this case they were the same. A market trader buying and selling in cash would show the same profit as the improvement in the bank balance. However, if a business sold on credit the profit would show much higher than the cash improvement as the customers had not yet paid. Put simply, the sales figure does not have to be paid for to be a sale although eventually it does otherwise it would be called a bad debt".

Ashna sent Jack away from that first meeting with a suggestion that he do the following:

- Think of a suitable trading name as Jack Whackhead clothing didn't seem to do it for her
- Open a separate bank account for all the business receipts and expenses so that business is kept separate from private matters
- Keep a good record of all transactions, particularly a cash book which should 'mirror' all the banking transactions

Jack did as he was asked and set up his company as Whack Jackhead Fashion Passion (WJFP & Co) and registered as self-employed with the HMRC (Her Majesty's Revenue and Customs). He was not sure about the & Co bit but he thought it sounded good and he had ideas bigger than just selling a few jumpers.

Sure enough with a lot of pain and aggravation, Jack got the company underway in a part-time basis and then one evening he decided to bite the bullet. He told his boss, Ben Crustybonce, what he thought of the job and that he was giving him a week's notice. To his surprise, Ben wished him luck and arranged a little works party for him on his last evening and presented him with a specially designed mug with his own picture on it. He was asleep in the picture as Ben felt that best represented him. Jack felt he must have completely misunderstood Ben as apart from his slightly pointed sense of humour, Ben also offered to try to help him with finding customers for his products.

So, WJFP & Co got off the ground and Jack wondered how he was going to make enough money to live. He managed it though and during the early part of the year he stopped selling direct to the public and decided to wholesale his own clothing. Through a contact from University, he went straight to one or two knitwear manufacturers from Eastern Europe and secured some excellent price deals on jumpers, He narrowly avoided being caught up in a money laundering operation as a drug cartel from Slovenia wanted him to 'lose' some of their cash. It was tempting but apart from being illegal, he fancied living for more than a week. He got out of the deal by pretending he was a bit crazy (easily done for Jack) by twitching and hiccoughing and talking gibberish every time the conversation started getting serious. Eventually, they got bored with it and when Jack finally went down on the ground retching, belching and holding his stomach they left and he hoped he would never see them again. Anyway, these products he sold with differing levels of mark-up depending on how he felt the market price was moving.

Jack found retailing customers who would buy jumpers 20 at a time from him and it seemed to be going well but he began to have financing difficulties by the end of the year and once again realised he needed Ashna's help so as soon as his year end came (he fixed it at June 30th with the tax authorities), he gave her a call, dropped off all his records and made an appointment to see her two weeks later.

Ashna produced a list of Income and Expenses as follows and suggested that as an exercise Jack should try to put an Income Statement together for his own company. He grunted but agreed as she knew what she was doing.

The Sales were £44,000 and he had incurred the following costs for the year:

| | £ |
|---|---|
| Cost of supplies from Europe | 33,000 |
| Purchase of a car (a right old banger!) | 5,000 |
| Rent & Rates of warehouse | 3,500 |
| Electricity | 800 |
| Motor & travel Expenses | 1,200 |
| Sundry expenses | 400 |
| Advertising & Printing | 930 |
| Bank Interest payable | 250 |

He had also taken drawings for himself of £6,000 out of the business bank account during the year and had inventory (stock of jumpers left at the year-end) of £4,200 value.

Hints:

- Deduct the closing inventory from the cost of supplies
- Work out the profit before the drawings
- Is the car purchase an operating expense? – (ignore for the income statement)

|                                  | £       | £       |
| -------------------------------- | ------- | ------- |
| Sales                            |         | 44,000  |
| Less Cost of Sales               |         |         |
| Cost of Supplies (Purchases)     | 33,000  |         |
| Less Closing Inventory           | -4,200  |         |
|                                  |         | -28,800 |
| Gross Profit                     |         | 15,200  |
|                                  |         |         |
| Less Overheads                   |         |         |
| Rent & Rates of warehouse        | 3,500   |         |
| Electricity                      | 800     |         |
| Motor & travel Expenses          | 1,200   |         |
| Sundry expenses                  | 400     |         |
| Advertising & Printing           | 930     |         |
| Bank Interest payable            | 250     |         |
| Total Overheads                  |         | -7,080  |
| Net Profit                       |         | 8,120   |
| Drawings (S/B on Balance Sheet)  |         | -6,000  |
| Surplus after Drawings           |         | £2,120  |

- The first point is that he had not sold all his supplies of jumpers and he still had unsold inventory of £4,200. This is deducted from the purchase of supplies as we are really only interested in what the cost of the actual sales are and not what he bought. If the closing inventory is deducted from the supplies purchased, the result will give us what supplies we have consumed.

- Secondly, the purchase of the car is what is known as a capital purchase. Like the closing inventory, it is still there at the year end and so should not be treated as if it has been consumed like all the other expenses.

- Thirdly, the profit is calculated before the drawings as this is the figure on which Jack is taxed whether he draws nothing or whether he draws a huge amount. The drawings are really shown on the next statement, the Balance Sheet, as a deduction from capital but is shown here to emphasise that the profit should be more than the drawings as otherwise the company might be in trouble.

"So I was doing all right" said Jack with the beginnings of a smile on his face for the first time.

"Well, yes and no" said Ashna. "You have made a profit and you have drawn less than the profit out of the business but you have also had to pay for £4,200 of inventory that you have not yet used and also bought a car for £5,000. The total of those is £9,200 and after accounting for the deduction of profit after drawings of £2,120 is £7,080. This sum in part explains why your bank has gone down. Presumably you had negotiated a bank overdraft which is why you are paying interest although if you could have gained more credit from some of your suppliers it would have been better?"

Once again, a ray of sunshine was passing across Jack's desert that he called a brain. That sum was nearly what his bank balance was. He had started with a £500 investment in the bank and it had fallen to over £6,000 overdraft – a fall of over £6,500! Another eureka moment for Jack.

Time for another lesson from Ashna. Oh dear. Just when he thought he was on top of it she gave him another scenario. What about in the second year when he would start with inventory in his warehouse? This would be the closing inventory from the previous year as whatever is in stock at the end of one year must by definition be in stock at the beginning of the next. It therefore needs to be adjusted as in the following example:

Suppose there is £20,000 in inventory in the warehouse at the beginning of the year and we make purchases of £57,000 during the year and there is inventory at the end of the year of £15,000. How much have we used to make the sales?

Jack was now beginning to get a vague idea of what she was on about. Clearly the inventory had gone down so the business must have used all the purchases plus £5,000 of the inventory in making the sales. In other words, the business had a cost of sales of £57,000 purchases plus £5,000 out of inventory making £62,000 in total. He mentioned this figure to Ashna more in hope than confidence.

She looked at him straight in the eyes and a huge smile came across her face as she raised both hands in the air and exclaimed "Geronimo. He's got it! You are bang on the money there. As the inventory has gone down you have not only used your purchases but also some more. If the inventory had increased then you would have used less to make the sales as some of the purchases had gone into inventory. You can simply use the formula of Opening Inventory add Purchases less Closing Inventory to arrive at the Cost of Sales." So she gave him another example to try:

"What is the gross profit from this group of figures? Purchases of goods for resale £27,000, Closing Inventory £6,200, Sales ££38,600 and Opening Inventory £8,000?"

He gave it a go and applied the formula for Cost of Sales she had told him.

Cost of Sales equals:

| | |
|---|---|
| Opening Inventory | £8,000 |
| Add Purchases | £27,000 |
| | £35,000 |
| Less Closing Inventory | -£6,200 |
| Cost of Sales | £28,800 |

Deduct this from the Sales of £38,600 and we have a gross profit of £9,800.

Once again, Ashna smiled at him and it seemed to hit him right in the chest. Was he starting to like this lady? She must have been 5 years older than him, which was unusual for him as he preferred girls much younger than himself as that made him feel more worldly when he was with them and he felt he did not need to act more mature than he really felt. He put it out of his mind - at least for the time being and besides which, she was probably married.

"Yes" she said. "Once again you are right and it would be shown like this."

| | | |
|---|---|---|
| Sales | | £38,600 |
| Less Cost of Sales | | |
| Opening Inventory | £8,000 | |
| Add Purchases | £27,000 | |
| | £35,000 | |
| Less Closing Inventory | -£6,200 | |
| Cost of Sales | | -£28,800 |
| Gross Profit | | £9,800 |

"From the gross profit is deducted the overheads to arrive at the Net Profit. This section from the sales down to the gross profit is known as the 'Trading Account'. You buy the goods for £28,800 and sell them for £38,600. It is the buy and sell or 'trading' part of the statement."

Jack was quickly developing a warm and cosy feeling towards Ashna and her voice sounded like birds fluttering in the branches of a willow tree and seemed to wash over him like warm oil. Had she drugged his coffee? What was wrong with him?

"Jack, Jack!" she said loudly. "Wake up. You look like you have had a dream about winning the lottery." He realised he had been dribbling a little and sucked in his breath to ensure he was not ejected from her office for weird and salacious behaviour.  Alas too late. Strings of dribble descended into his lap which he quickly covered up with an old envelope from Ashna's desk and he thought he had got away with it. Ashna was on a roll now and decided she would give Jack another push.

"Jack, suppose your business grows and you decide to manufacture the goods yourself, you might have the following costs. Sales £200,000, Opening Inventory £34,000, Purchases £100,000, Closing Inventory £57,500, you also have wages paid to the people who make the garments of £52,000 and you pay a part-time book-keeper £7,400. You pay £6,300 in other overheads so how should this all be shown."

Jack made his usual grunting sound and proceeded to arrive at the gross profit and deduct all the other costs as follows:

| | £ | £ |
|---|---|---|
| Sales | | £200,000 |
| Less Cost of Sales | | |
| Opening Inventory | £34,000 | |
| Add Purchases | £100,000 | |
| | £134,000 | |
| Less Closing Inventory | -£57,500 | |
| Cost of Sales | | -£76,500 |
| Gross Profit | | £123,500 |
| Less Expenses | | |
| Total Wages | £59,400 | |
| Other overheads | £6,300 | -£65,700 |
| Net Profit before drawings | | £57,800 |

Ashna started by saying he had the right answer for the profit but that is not how it should be shown and that it should be as follows:

| | £ | £ |
|---|---|---|
| Sales | | 200,000 |
| Less Cost of Sales | | |
| Opening Inventory | 34,000 | |
| Add Purchases | 100,000 | |
| | 134,000 | |
| Less Closing Inventory | (57,500) | |
| Purchases consumed | 76,500 | |
| Direct Wages | 52,000 | |
| Cost of Sales | | (128,500) |
| Gross Profit | | 71,500 |
| Less Expenses | | |
| Indirect Wages | 7,400 | |
| Other overheads | 6,300 | (13,700) |
| Net Profit before drawings | | 57,800 |

"I can see that you have separated the wages with the Direct Wages showing above the Gross Profit figure. Why is that?" said Jack, a little abashed as he had thought he had done it rather well.

Ashna explained, "The first thing is the difference between Direct and Indirect Wages (more about this later in Costings). The direct wages are the wages of the people who actually make the product or provide the service. In this case the £52,000 paid for the makers of the garments would be direct wages as they are directly attributable to the individual products. These are added on to the Purchases of cloth, after adjusting for the inventory changes, to arrive at the cost of sales. In other words, the cost of sales is now not just the £76,000 that you had but £76,000 plus £52,000 making £128,500. Additionally, the book-keeper's wages would be classified as Indirect wages and would show in the general overheads and expenses. This means that the gross profit would not be £123,500 but £71,500."

Jack needed a smoke but decided he would not score any brownie points with Ashna if he tried to light up. "Why have you also used brackets rather than the minus sign?"

"Aha" said Ashna. "There is a sound historical reason for this. Brackets emphasise more the negative figures and they were used in the past because there were many errors created when accounts were done in manuscript and the minus sign was slightly misplaced or a 'T' was crossed in the wrong place turning a positive figure into a negative where the cross was placed as a minus. The custom has remained and you must admit it does emphasise the negative figures well, even in printed figures?" She had a little twinkle in her eye when she said this as she clearly wanted Jack to accept her authority on the subject.

Jack decided not to speak further on this topic as he wanted to keep on the right side of her. He decided to go for it. "How about you and I going out for dinner sometime if you have a free evening?"

For the first time Ashna was a little taken aback and instinctively rebuffed him rather quickly. "I don't think we know each other well enough and also I try to avoid going out with clients. How do you know I am not married anyway?"

"So sorry. I..I..I didn't mean to offend you" said Jack with a suitable grovelling tone but inwardly he was smiling as he had found out that Ashna was unmarried. Did she have a boyfriend? He did not care. After all, he sort of had a girlfriend but he felt a strong connection with Ashna which seemed to go beyond her useful financial advice.

"The next meeting we had better stick to the second of the accounting statements called the Balance Sheet." She was a little subdued when she said this as he detected she had been thrown off balance by his brazen invitation. He really hoped her big beaming smile would return for their next meeting.

Meanwhile she had given him some material to pore over. It was all about accounting concepts, what is a cost and how costs are spread across accounting periods.

*More practice Questions and Answers on this chapter in Appendices Part 2.*

## Key Chapter Points

1. What the main accounting statements are -

- Income statement - this summarises trading transactions between two balance sheet dates and is based on accrued income and expenses

- Balance sheet - this summarises the assets and liabilities at one point in time

- Cash Flow Statement – this reconciles the profit made in the period to the movement in the bank balance

- Budgets - projected income, costs and cash requirements

2. Who uses these statements and why? Stakeholders – Primary & Secondary

- For managing the company, for borrowing from the bank, shareholder returns etc.

3. Detail of an Income Statement

Main sections - trading a/c is part to gross profit. Less overheads giving profit.

It shows the profit earned on the sales and how well a company has traded over a period of time

4. Terms used

Sales – turnover, Cost of Sales, Gross Profit, Overheads, Operating Profit,

# 3. Accounting Concepts and Cost Categories

Jack got home that night and poured himself a drop of the amber nectar from the fridge. That is lager for the uninitiated. He liked a cold one now and again although he doubted whether it would help him to understand the information that Ashna had given him. It all seemed a bit theoretical about what is a cost etc.

The first section was on 'accounting concepts'. Now there's an expression to turn the strongest man to jelly.

Apparently accounts are drawn up on the basis of four main accounting concepts (although there are others). These being:

1. Going concern basis

2. Consistency concept

3. Prudence Concept

4. Accruals or matching concept

The 'Going Concern' concept means that we assume the business is going to continue as a 'going concern' and therefore the assets will be valued at their value to the business owner rather than their value if the business closed down. Obviously, if the business was going to close even Jack could see that many of the items would not fetch their perceived value. For instance, Jack doubted he could sell his stock of clothing at the price he paid for them if he had to close down and sell them quickly. Well, that made some sense so he assumed if you did know it was closing down that many of the figures would change for the worse which would explain why so many companies could not pay their suppliers when they closed down.

The 'Consistency' concept means consistently applying an accounting policy the same way each year. This means that if you value inventory at the year-end in a certain way, such as taking 20% off for those that will not sell or using a depreciation method then it should be applied consistently in the same way. This makes sense again as otherwise you could show different profits each year when it suited you.

The 'Prudence' concept is about being prudent or cautious when placing values on items. For instance, if you buy a gold bar for £112 and at the year-end it is worth £120 you still show it as £112 as you have not actually made the profit until it is sold. However, if the gold bar fell in value to £95 then it should be shown in the accounts as £95. In other words, you take it on the chin when there is a perceived loss but when there appears to be a profit, you keep the value at its cost and not its selling price.

The 'Accruals' concept is also known as the matching concept or apportionment concept. This means that transactions are recognised when they occur not when cash changes hands. So if your year-end is 30th June and you pay rent of £900 for a photocopier in May that runs from June 1st to August 31st, then you have actually only used one month of the rent (June) during the financial year and the other two months belongs in the next financial year. As at the year-end on June 30th, you have actually 'prepaid' two months. So the cost would be 'apportioned' as £300 (1 month) for the current year and £600 (2 months) for the next year. This £600 is called a 'prepayment' and is effectively owed back to you at the year end. The reverse is also true of a bill that is received and paid after the year end that relates to the current year. Ashna very kindly had created an example for Jack to work out as follows:

If you had 5 electricity bills over the period of just over a year what would be the charge for electricity for the year ended 31 12 2014?

3 months ended    28 02 14   £7,500

3 months ended    31 05 14   £4,000

3 months ended    31 08 14   £3,000

3 months ended    30 11 14   £4,800

3 months ended    28 02 15   £8,400

Jack decided he needed another cold one and carried his empty can back towards the bin and tripped sending it sailing through the air into the goldfish bowl. As his face hurtled towards the floor he could have sworn that the goldfish, actually it was a shubunkin as it had long fins and a long flowing tail, seemed to have a smile on his face. He assumed it was a 'he' as otherwise it would not have a smile on its face when faced with a lager meteorite. He fished it out of the bowl, glared at the fish which he had named Shuggie and grabbed beer number two. Back to the question. He realised that he could just add all the bills up and take 12 months worth out of the 15 months. That might give him an idea but then he saw a little note from Ashna which read "look at the first and the last quarters." Aha. Now he understood. The middle three bills had all been consumed during the year and amounted to £11,800. The other two he assumed needed to be apportioned. The first bill for £7,500 had two months in this year and one in the previous year so that would be 2/3 or £5,000 relating to this year. The last bill for £8,400 was similar except one month or 1/3 relates to this year amounting to £2,800. The total usage of electricity would therefore be £5,000 plus £11,800 plus £2,800 = £19,600. He later found out that he was correct and also that the last month of £2,800 would be called an 'accrual' which is a bill you have not received during the year. At the year-end it might even be an estimate but it needs to be 'accrued' or allowed for. So much for accounting concepts.

The next area of notes covered what is a cost or an overhead. Firstly, anything you buy or use up is a cost. If it is all used during the year such as electricity, purchases (apart from inventory), wages, promotion expenses, motor expenses etc., it is known as an operating or revenue cost in that it is all deducted from the revenue to arrive at the profit. If it still remains at the year-end and has not been purchased with the intention to resell it, it would be classified as a capital cost and will therefore show in the Balance Sheet. "In other words" thought Jack, "if you buy it and use it up it will be in the income statement but if it is still there at the year end, it will be an asset in the Balance Sheet." He knew they were looking at Balance Sheets tomorrow. "So" he thought, "if I buy a machine for £20,000 and it is still there at the end of the year it will classify as capital expenditure. He learnt that everything you buy gets deducted from the sales to arrive at the profit. Revenue costs are knocked off in full straightaway but capital costs are knocked off over a period of their life. This is called depreciation (also examined later).

The last section of notes dealt with overheads. Overheads (or expenses) are the running costs of a business. They are not a part of the basic product such as the raw materials in the product or the wages of the people who make the products but you need to spend them to keep the business going. Examples of these would be all the office running costs such as rent and rates, heat and light, cleaning, telephone, computer maintenance (not the computer itself), There would also be selling costs such as motoring and travel, advertising and promotion, commission paid for a sale and website costs. Then there are distribution costs such as warehousing, special packaging, transport or carriage costs. Finance costs of loans and overdraft would be another overhead. The loan itself would not classify as a cost and neither would the annual repayment amount of the loan but the interest on the loan would be.

Jack had thankfully finished the notes and got a pretty good grasp of them. Unfortunately, he had also finished his second beer which had put him in a very mellow state. He decided to go for it and break his weekday rule of never having more than two beers. It was a huge mistake. The first can that he had drunk was placed right next to Shuggie, the shubunkin. His shirt touched it as he walked past and as he tried to grab it as it was falling, he clouted Shuggie's bowl. For a very small period of time, everything seemed to stand still and then the bowl ever so slowly slid off its counter top. As it fell to the floor, Jack launched himself at it and failed to catch it. The bowl shattered, sending shards of glass flying in all directions including one into Jack's hand. He did not notice it at first as he was so busy trying to pick up a very irritated, flapping Shuggie off the tiled floor. He got him into another spare cooking bowl and quickly filled it with water. Shuggie seemed O.K. as although he had no great emotional ties to him, he had won him at a fairground during a fun night out with an old girlfriend. It was then that he saw the blood. His hand was pouring blood from the glass cut so he wrapped a cloth around it and decided he needed a trip to A&E (Accident and Emergency at the hospital). 3 hours later he got home after a few stitches in his thumb to find Shuggie staring at him as if nothing had happened. He would have to find someone who really liked goldfish!

_More practice Questions and Answers on this chapter in Appendices Part 2._

## Key Chapter Points

- Four Key Concepts - Going concern basis, Consistency, Prudence and Accruals (also called apportionment or matching concept)
- Two types of cost – operating which is a running cost (used up) and is in the income statement – capital cost which is purchased to help the business expand and is still there at the year-end but subject to depreciation over its lifetime

# 4.    The Balance Sheet

Thankfully for Jack, Ashna was happy to arrange another meeting the next day and they met in a coffee bar called Grinder's late morning which was a good time for Jack as he had filled himself up with a cholesterol sandwich from the caravan up the road, had a smoke and was feeling at one with the world although he was a little concerned about how Ashna would receive him after he had put his foot in his big mouth more than once on the previous day. He would have to explain his bandaged thumb as well.

He arrived first and found a nice, large wooden table with plenty of room on after he had pushed the sugar bowl, menus and other coloured leaflets to one side. He sat in his usual slumped fashion with his hair hanging down over his eyes and cheeks so he did not see her arrive until she was right by his table. He looked up and saw the vision that was Ashna. She had that huge smile back on her face and looked so cute in her business suit and carrying her smart burgundy-leather briefcase. He was momentarily speechless. A rare event for Jack but he soon recovered.

"The drinks are on me," he said expansively and rather too loud. In fact, he embarrassed himself as what was supposed to be super cool turned out to make him appear like a mad man who could not control himself. The right cheek on Ashna's face twitched a little as she fought back a laugh and he then repeated his statement in a much softer voice. She opted for a cappuccino with a sprinkle and no sugar. He could have guessed the no sugar bit as she seemed to have the trimmest figure he had ever seen and her posture in the rather stiff chair was that of a model on a film shot for the promotion of Jimmy Choo's or Aquascutum. He ordered the coffee and it was delivered to his table by a waiter (with a name tag of Wally – appropriate!) who looked like he did not want to do the job, so a tip was out of the question although even when Jack was short he usually tipped at least 10% as he remembered how hard he worked for his minimum wage in a restaurant.

"So" commenced Ashna. "The Balance Sheet beckons. I had better start by describing it to you. It is a summary of what you own (Assets) and what you owe (Liabilities). Unlike the Income Statement which summarises your sales and costs over a period of time, the Balance Sheet is a statement at a point in time. Your assets and liabilities are changing daily as you sell things and buy things so the Balance Sheet is drawn up at the end of the Income Statement period. So, if your Income Statement is for the year ending 31.3 2013, your Balance Sheet will be drawn up 'as at' 31.3.2013. Therefore the Income Statement runs up to the Balance Sheet date. It is only true on that date so it is a snapshot at a point in time. It tells you how stable you are and what money you have and what you owe others. Also, what assets like cars or stock you own."

"Aha," cut in Jack, "so it is like a summary of my financial position at a point in time."

"Exactly. In fact the newer terminology is to call it a Statement of Financial Position (or SOFP) but the expression Balance Sheet is so universally known that I cannot see it being replaced colloquially for many years even though on the published accounts of Public Companies it is called a SOFP."

"So what does mine look like then?" asked Jack excitedly.

"Well, I think we should just go over the five main headings first and then it will make a bit of sense. They are easy to learn as they are your long and short term assets, your long and short term liabilities and your capital. Let's deal with them one at a time.

The long term assets are called Non-Current Assets (also formerly and still commonly known as Fixed Assets). These are the assets not used in trading such as buildings you own, cars, machinery etc. the assumption is that they are there at the end of the year and you have not used them up."

"Why are they called something they are not?" asked Jack with a bewildered expression.

"What do you mean?"

"Well, they are called Non-Current Assets, right? So you might as well call them Non-bananas because they are not bananas." Jack laughed at his own humour but quickly stopped as Ashna gave him a glare as she carried on.

"The short term assets are known as Current Assets. These are assets used in the trading cycle of the business such as Inventories (stocks), Accounts Receivable (money due from customers, often called Debtors) and money in the bank or held on the premises in cash form (known as petty cash). The total of these two sections, which are arranged under each other, are known as the Total Assets, not surprisingly. This total will always equal the total of the remaining three headings." She waited for Jack to make a silly comment and as he opened his mouth she muttered "Don't go down there" so he closed his mouth again with his lips making a popping sound as they plopped together.

"Now we have the other three headings and the first one is the Capital Account. This shows the original capital (usually money but could be another asset like a van) that has been put into the company in the first place. Added to that will be the profit made during the year and any drawings out by the owner are deducted. This is because the profit effectively adds to the company's capital and the drawings reduce it. So, your opening capital was what, Jack?"

Jack was thinking how magnificent she looked today especially when in full flow as she was now.

She asked him again and he said it was £500 that he started with.

"Right, so your opening capital was £500 and your opening Balance Sheet would have been shown as follows:

<u>Assets</u> : Cash at bank £500 and <u>Capital</u>: £500

So the cash at the bank in the beginning was also the capital invested.

Now what has happened to your capital account? Well, from your original figures you have made a profit of £8,120 and you made drawings of £6,000 so your capital account would be shown as follows:

| | |
|---|---|
| Opening Capital | £500 |
| <u>Add</u> Profit for Year | £8,120 |
| | £8,620 |
| <u>Less</u> Drawings | £6,000 |
| Closing Capital | £2,620 |

This closing capital would be your opening capital for the next year so it moves up or down depending on your level of profit and drawings. If you make a loss, this would reduce your capital like the drawings do."

Jack was thinking that it made a lot of sense. "But what if I am running short of money and had to put more cash, say, £1,000 into the company?"

"Good question Jack. What is your best guess on how to treat it?"

"I guess it is just like increasing the capital. So the capital would go up by £1,000 as would the bank."

Ashna giggled in delight as she realised she was getting through to him. She was a natural teacher as she seemed to get as much or more pleasure out of teaching Jack as out of doing the figures. She rather liked Jack when he was not playing the fool. "The capital account would now look like this:

| | |
|---|---|
| Opening Capital | £500 |
| Add Profit for Year | £8,120 |
| | £8,620 |
| Add Capital Introduced | £1,000 |
| | £9,620 |
| Less Drawings | £6,000 |
| Closing Capital | £3,620 |

So the closing capital has also increased by £1,000."

Jack felt he was on a roll. "Can I try to summarise it, please? I start with the Original Capital in the company. I add on any profit or deduct any loss and add on any further capital introduced and deduct any drawings."

"That's great, Jack. Now let's look at the other two headings - the long and short-term liabilities. The long term liabilities are (like the long term assets) known as 'Non-Current' Liabilities. By long term is meant not due to be paid within the next 12 months. So effectively this covers one main item which is any loans from a bank. A loan from a bank is different from an overdraft in that the bank actually lends you a sum of money which is then put into your ordinary bank account in much the same way as you putting in your own money. There are other long-term liabilities such as Finance Leases but these we shall look at later. The last heading is short term liabilities known as Current Liabilities. These are any bills needed to be paid within 12 months. There are two main items here. One is the Accounts Payable (money due to suppliers, often called Creditors) and the other is any bank overdraft. So a company will either have money in the bank – a Current Asset or it will owe the bank – a Current Liability.

There we have it, Jack. All the elements of a Balance Sheet. Now let's see if you can put yours together?"

Jack did not like the way this was going as he thought he was employing an accountant to do this for him. He felt like saying so but if she had not been so pretty in her business suit he would have as well.

"O.K., you have a car costing £5,000, you have Inventory of £4,200 and you are also owed £4,320 by your customers. You have already done your capital account (£500 initial investment, profit of £8,120 and drawings of £6,000). You have no loans but you owe your suppliers £4,600 and you have a bank overdraft of £6,300."

Jack thought for a while and then proceeded to ask Ashna if she would like another coffee. He thought a deflective strategy might work but alas!

"I would love one Jack but my turn. You carry on with the calculation and I shall get the coffee. What coffee do you fancy?"

He asked for a double Espresso as staying awake whilst doing accounts was his goal and he really wanted to impress Ashna. She left the table to find Wally the waiter as he seemed to have taken a magic course in body evaporation. Meanwhile Jack produced the following after much effort:

| ASSETS | | |
|---|---|---|
| Non-Current Assets | | |
| Car | | £5,000 |
| Current Assets | | |
| Inventories | £4,200 | |
| Accounts Receivable | £4,320 | |
| | | 8,520 |
| Total Assets | | £13,520 |
| | | |
| CAPITAL & LIABILITIES | | |
| Capital a/c | | |
| Opening Capital | £500 | |
| Profit in Year | £8,120 | |
| | 8,620 | |
| Drawings | (6,000) | |
| Closing Capital | | £2,620 |
| LOANS | | - |
| CURRENT LIABILITIES | | |
| Accounts Payable | £4,600 | |
| Bank Overdraft | £6,300 | |
| | | £10,900 |
| Total Capital & Liabilities | | £13,520 |

She came back with the coffees and could not believe her eyes. He had done it perfectly. "Well done Jack. You have got how the profit shown on the Income Statement is then transferred to the Capital A/C in the Balance Sheet as we discussed before. Sometimes the Balance Sheet is summarised in what is known as 'the Accounting Equation' which is Assets – Liabilities = Capital. In this case it would be £13,520 - £10,900 = £2,620.

The Capital is effectively what the company would fetch if you sold all the assets and paid off all the liabilities. It is sometimes known as the Net Worth or Balance Sheet value. Of course a company might sell for more than its Balance Sheet value because it is highly profitable or growing well or have a great brand value, for instance."

Jack's ears pricked up. "So if WJ&Co built up its net assets to, say, £30 million, it might sell for even more because of its great reputation for quality or value?"

"Absolutely right but I think we should have a little chat about the Current Assets and Current Liabilities as this is a critical part of your finance problem." That brought him down to earth.

Jack dived into his double Espresso and was quietly preening himself after his praise from Ashna. She certainly seemed to be happy when he did something well. "OK then. Let's go for it"

"The Current Assets should always be more than the Current Liabilities. In fact, they should be approaching double. The Current Assets less the Current Liabilities are known as the Net Current Assets or 'working capital'. The figure itself means little on its own as a large multi-national will need millions in its working capital and a small corner shop will need very little. How much do you have, Jack?"

Jack surveyed his current situation. "Well, the Current Assets are £8,520 and the Current Liabilities are £10,900 so I appear to have a negative figure of £2,380 ........ That does not look good but I do not have to pay the bank off straightaway so I really only owe £6,300."

"Sorry Jack but you have to assume that the bank might 'call in' their overdraft at any moment and right now you are in the hands of the bank. Also, your Inventories are £4,200 and that is not money coming in soon necessarily"

"So I am up the creek without a paddle then!"

"Well, only if you do nothing about it. What you really need to do is find some other long term money and the simplest way is to go to the bank and ask for a loan over 3 years of, say, £6,000 and that would nearly remove your overdraft and give you some room to manoeuvre. In other words, you should ask the bank to replace your overdraft with a loan but, of course, all loans need to be repaid and if it is over 3 years then that would be approximately £2,000 per year plus interest so you would need to convince the bank that you are generating enough profit to repay it. You would also need to keep some overdraft facility with the bank to allow for fluctuations in your cash position."

"Good. We have done then. So I need to get a loan or maybe another investor like my Dad if he is crazy enough and then move it on from there."

"I don't think he would need to be crazy to invest in you Jack. You have a lot to offer. You are certainly quick with figures and you can negotiate and despite how you try to still portray yourself as a laid back student type you have a great deal of charm." She immediately regretted saying that as it seemed to come out wrong and she became all flustered and stammered "What I m...m...mean is that you should be able to s... s...sell well to your customers."

She became even more agitated and Jack was sure he noticed a bit of a pink flush come up on her cheeks. Jack thought he would let her off the hook although he was sure she had a soft spot for him which was not six feet down at the bottom of the garden.

"I understand. I know I am a good wheeler-dealer but I would like to take it further as I want to build a business for life not just to pay my wages this year. Is there anything else we should cover today?"

"Not today" said Ashna. "But we do need to examine one other relevant item called 'depreciation'. Do you know what that is?"

"I guess it is when something becomes worth less over time."

"Quite right. So please give me a ring when you are next free for a meeting, Jack as this topic needs to be examined quickly before you forget what we have already covered."

They got up and walked out of the coffee bar as Wally the waiter decided he would show his face, presumably feeling he was due some sort of gratuity. No way until hell freezes over thought Jack as he walked just behind Ashna and he appeared like a huge shambling abominable snowman next to her dainty figure. Jack had an overwhelming desire to look after her as she was so petite and he even opened the door for her. He had been taught good manners by his parents but often felt it was a show of submission to adopt them. However, on this occasion he just wanted to. Ashna turned to him with a glare as she obviously was of the opinion that she could open the door herself and then her face softened when she saw the pitiful look of eagerness on Jack's face. With a parting smile she left him with the impatient click clacking of her shoes on the pavement sounding in his ears. He went on his way dragging his worn heels with a strange, unexplainable feeling of loss.

_**More practice Questions and Answers on this chapter in Appendices Part 2.**_

## Key Chapter Points

1. The Balance Sheet (also known as the SOFP) is a position statement at a single point of time.
2. The layout of a SOFP is essentially a complicated layout of two columns of figures named assets and liabilities.
3. The assets which you own less the liabilities which you owe equate to the capital from the investors plus any accumulated profits.
4. There are five major headings in a SOFP – Non-Current or Fixed Assets, Current Assets, Long Term Liabilities (Creditors due > 12 months), Current Liabilities (Creditors due < 12 months), Capital a/c (capital invested plus profits less drawings)
5. The Balance Sheet shows the Net Worth of a company, its borrowings and assets and whether or not it is stable. It is an essential statement for a banker to assess any security (collateral) for a loan.

# 5.    Depreciation

In the two weeks since he had last seen Ashna his business had really taken off with a big increase in orders so he had put off ringing her. He had also pranged his car. Actually, somebody else had pranged it. He had been cruising around a supermarket car park looking for a suitable space in which his old convertible SAAB could reside when bang! Some half crazed nitwit decided to reverse out of his parking spot without so much as a backward glance and straight into the side of his beloved banger. It had been a nice day up until then. The sun was out and he had his hood down and the stereo was playing, at high volume, a great guitar riff from Muse's Plug In Baby track when it happened. That was not the worst of it. This little ginger haired gnome like gonk came out of his highly polished Mercedes and proceeded to throw his inadequate weight around in a loud voice trying to give the impression that as Jack was a 'student type' it was clearly his fault. Jack suggested that his new found gnome like friend admit to being in the wrong and they could then let the insurance companies do the work. Not good enough for gnome like Merc man. He seemed to want blood. He then kicked out at Jack's car putting a further denge in the side and proceeded to swear and cuss in an appalling manner. Jack let him go on for 5 minutes and then he turned the guy around and grabbed him by the seat of his pants and his jacket collar and bodily stuffed him slowly head first through his open Merc side window. There was a lot of clapping in the car park, particularly from young mothers who had been covering their children's ears when his foul tirade started. This was too much for ginger, gnome-like, gonky Merc man and he grabbed his mobile and muttered about the police. However, before he did I found I had several witnesses who would happily testify as to whose fault it was. He realised that he was onto a loser so went off to no doubt berate his wife or secretary or someone on whom he could vent his spleen.' LAHOO.....ZAHAR!' thought

Jack. He was lucky at the end of it and he realised that if Merc man had not used such foul language none of the witnesses would have been bothered to come forward. They told him as much. Anyway he realised he knew something about depreciation when he looked at his poor car. The red go-faster stripe down the side was now very wobbly and two panels were well caved in. He decided to call Ashna as he needed a lift. A psychological one not a physical one as his car was still roadworthy.

They agreed to meet again at Grinder's Coffee House mid-morning and this time Ashna beat him there. He had washed and shaved this time and was looking almost presentable (or so he thought). She, on the other hand, was again a veritable mirage. Dressed in figure hugging jeans and a dark green polo shirt she looked good enough to eat. He just refrained from saying so and the coffees were ordered again from Wally the waiter. He still looked disinterested but was at least trying a little.

"So how has your week been going?" chirped Ashna.

Jack recounted the story of his car prang and Ashna nearly fell off her seat she was laughing so hard after he told her about stuffing Merc man through his car window. That created an easy going start to their meeting and straightaway Ashna launched herself into a chat about depreciation.

"It is a reduction in value of an asset over the period and only applies to Non-Current Assets. In other words when you buy a car for £20,000 ...."

"I wish" cut in Jack

"When you buy a car for £20,000, it is still there at the end of the year but you have actually used up some of its value – let's say £4,000. That £4,000 is shown as an overhead cost in the Income Statement, even though you do not pay it to anybody, so the profit will show as £4,000 less. At the same time the car will not show in the Non-Current Assets as £20,000 but as £20,000 - £4,000 = £16,000 being the new current value at the year end. In other words there are two aspects or entries in the books to record depreciation. The costs are increased by the depreciation for the year and the Asset is decreased in value by the same figure."

"Sounds good but who determines the amount of depreciation?"

"Very perceptive question, Jack. It is actually agreed between the Finance Director and the external auditor in a large organisation so basically you would take your direction from me."

"Anytime baby." Once again Jack had stepped over the mark. It was not that Jack had used rather suggestive language but he had thrown her out of her teaching mode.

"Jack, did your mother drop you on your head when you were born because you seem incapable of concentrating for more than a few minutes." Jack wondered that himself sometimes, particularly after his fourth beer.

"There are two main methods of depreciation. The simplest is called the straight line method. It is called that because it is an equal amount each year and would show as a straight line if shown in graphical form. If we say the car costs £20,000 and will last 4 years then divide the cost by the number of years to arrive at the yearly depreciation. This gives £20,000/4 = £5,000. So this would be the depreciation each year and the value of the car or Net Book Value (NBV) would decrease by £5,000. It would show as follows:

| Cost | £20,000 |
|---|---|
| Dep'n Year 1 | 5,000 |
| NBV Year 1 | 15,000 |
| Depn Year 2 | 5,000 |
| NBV Year 2 | 10,000 |

And so on to year 4 where the Net Book Value would be zero."

Jack grasped this pretty well. "So presumably if we estimated the car to last 5 years then the depreciation would be £20,000/5 = £4,000 per year so that would be less of a cost each year making your profits higher?"

Ashna was constantly amazed by Jack's insight. He seemed so dozy and laid back sometimes that he appeared almost asleep and then he comes out with something like this. "You've got it Jack but it all equals out in the end when the vehicle is sold as any under or over estimate will be put right then. Sometimes you might only want to keep the car or machine for a set time rather than for its whole life and you may estimate a scrap sale value and this changes the calculation. Let's try one Jack. Suppose you buy a machine for a contract which will last 3 years. The machine costs you £45,000 and you expect to sell it for £15,000 after three years. What would be the depreciation each year using the straight line method?" Ashna thought she had fixed him with this one.

Jack made some peculiar grunting noises and got out his biro and notepad and scribbled a few figures on it and then said £10,000 to Ashna.

She assumed it was a lucky guess and asked him to justify it. "OK. The machine costs £45,000 and is presumed sold for £15,000 so over its life it must depreciate £45,000 - £15,000 = £30,000. If this is spread over three years it would be £30,000/3 = £10,000 per year."

She almost leapt out of her seat as if she had found a nugget of gold. Wally the waiter appeared at the time and Ashna's head caught the underside of his tray and sent all his glasses and cups flying across the room. Ashna was very apologetic and Wally, in line with his general lack of enthusiasm for life, appeared quite unmoved. Jack was secretly very pleased as he was the one usually making a scene. "It's catching, isn't it?" he mocked. Ashna was already more than a little distraught but knew what he meant. "Don't worry, be happy" he sang in best Bob Marley tones. At that she laughed and all was returned to normal.

"You obviously understand that one but there is one more method to be aware of called the 'Reducing Balance' method. With this method you pick a percentage to apply to calculate the depreciation but rather than applying it to the cost you apply it to the 'reduced' balance i.e. the Net Book Value. So our £20,000 car we might pick a percentage of 25% (a commonly used one for cars) and the calculations for each year would look as follows:

| | |
|---|---:|
| Cost | £20,000 |
| Dep'n Year 1 (25% of Cost) | 5,000 |
| NBV Year 1 | 15,000 |
| Depn Year 2 (25% of 15,000) | 3,750 |
| NBV Year 2 | 11,250 |
| Depn Year 3 (25% of 11,250) | 2,812 |
| NBV Year 3 | 8,438 |

And so on, so the balance will never go down to zero.

The percentage chosen will reflect how long you think the asset will have great value. For instance, plant and machinery will last a long time so you might pick 10% whereas IT equipment you might pick 50%. The big advantage of this method is that it puts greater depreciation in the earlier years as compared to the straight line method which has the same figure each year."

"So how do we know which method to pick?" The maths seemed straightforward to Jack but it all seemed conceptually a little hit and miss.

"Firstly, you do not have to have the same method for every category of asset. For instance, you might pick 25% reducing balance for vehicles and straight line over 7 years for machinery. This is an example of an accounting policy in that you have a choice as to how you do it. You should, however, always keep the same method for each type of asset. Secondly, the method chosen is often custom and practice (like 25% Reducing Balance for cars). Thirdly, you pick a method and time period (or percentage) that suits the life of the Asset. A building you might depreciate over 50 years for instance."

Jack mused on this. "Surely, if you pick a very high depreciation method then you will show less profit and pay less tax?"

"Actually, Jack that is a good point. However, in the UK, HMRC (Her Majesty's Revenue and Customs) do not like accounting policies and have one of their own so they actually add back anything you deduct in depreciation and deduct their own version of depreciation called capital allowances. These are the same across all companies. The effect is that the taxable profit is a different profit to what is shown."

"That's a bit complicated. I think I shall consign that one to the 'buried deep' part of my memory." He was losing it on this one.

"Agreed, I should not worry about it. Just try to fix a fair rate for your depreciation policy. So, anything else I can help you with Jack or should we call it a day for the time being?"

"Appen uz lark we be well stitched fo now" said Jack.

Ashna was extremely puzzled. She was not sure if Jack was being rude or she had just misheard him. "I'm sorry, what was that."

Now it was Jack's turn to laugh. In fact he threw his head back and made a big guffawing sound and Ashna smiled at him more with sympathy than amusement. "Just giving you a bit of Lancashire dialect which basically means we are OK and done now. It is a bit like Jive talk for folks from Lancashire"

"I didn't know you were from Lancashire."

"I'm not. I just like the local lingo"

"All right" said Ashna. "Time I was on my way" She headed off and Jack immediately felt a constriction in his chest as she walked out of the door. "What is that?" he thought as he had never felt this close to someone before. He hung around for another coffee just long enough to see Wally the waiter being given a massive rocket by the coffee shop owner and it looked like he was in the process of being fired. He overheard him haranguing Wally about dropping the tray so Jack felt he should step in. Although Wally was not his favourite waiter on the planet, he was by no means the worst.

"Excuse me" butted in Jack "It is unfair to treat Wally this way as it was absolutely not his fault. My friend leapt up from her seat without looking and hit his tray with her head. Wally could do nothing about it."

Wally turned to Jack with a tear in his eye. "It's alright, Sir, the boss is quite right to fire me as I am not cut out for this job but thanks anyway." Wally took off his apron and the owner went into his till and paid him up for what he was due. As he was walking out, Jack asked him over to his table and beckoned him to a seat.

"Why did you look so upset when I was talking to the owner?" asked Jack gently.

"It was nothing to do with being fired as it has happened before but nobody has ever stood up for me my whole life and that is the first time so I am really grateful." This now bought a tear to Jack's eye, which he was careful to conceal and he was beginning to understand a bit about why Wally's motivation was on the low side. He had no self-esteem at all.

"Surely your Mum or Dad stood up for you over something?"

"No, never. My Dad was always out drinking and my Mum worked most nights at the hospital so I hardly saw her and when I did she was tired out. I used to row with my Dad as he expected her to put his food on the table even though she was so tired. He even hit me a couple of times after he had been drinking."

"You must hate him"

"No not really. He did not mean it and it was really the drink that did it as well as him being laid off from the steel works. My parents have split up now and I now live with my elder sister. Unfortunately, I am struggling to help with my share of the rent now."

Jack was silent for quite some time. People did not normally unload like this to him in coffee bars. Then a thought struck him like a bolt of lightning.

"Wally"

"Yes"

"Do you like clothing?"

"Well, yes of course, otherwise I would be arrested" Wally was not trying to be funny.

"No, I don't mean do you like wearing it. I just mean does it interest you as a product?"

"Well, I like some of Balmain's stuff but I'm very unsure about Yves St Laurent's design direction since he died. Gaultier is great as I have always thought he epitomises what is best about French Haute Couture. Paul Smith also does for me with his casual menswear." His eyes looked bright as he spoke.

"Where did you pick this knowledge up from? "The hair on the back of Jack's neck started to prickle and he just had that feeling there was more to Wally than being a rubbish waiter.

"Oh my sister is a clothing designer and I developed an interest from that I suppose."

"You suppose" exclaimed Jack. "Wally, I am trying to develop a clothing distribution channel through wholesaling but it is growing at quite a rate and I cannot cope with it all. I barely have enough wages for myself but at the rate it is growing, I cannot cope but most of the work needed is routine such as packaging, making deliveries etc. How would you like to join me?"

Wally was almost crying now and he could not speak but nodded his agreement.

"Hang on. You do not know what I am paying you or even if I can afford you."

Wally found his tongue at last. "Look, if you will stand up for me like you did before, I cannot see you dumping on me. Anyway, what have I got to lose? I don't have a job any more. The least I can do is give it a good go."

They shook hands and so Wally became Jack's first employee but that night Jack had no idea how he would pay him.

*More practice Questions and Answers on this chapter in Appendices Part 2.*

## Key Chapter Points

- Depreciation is a means of spreading the cost of a Non-Current Asset (Fixed Asset) over its useful life
- It is a notional cost and so does not affect cash flow
- Cost of asset less Depreciation gives the Net Book Value (NBV)
- Two main methods of depreciation - Straight Line and Reducing Balance

# 6.    Double Entry Book-keeping

The next morning Jack got up and immediately arranged an appointment with his bank. Not only was he not earning enough but he needed to pay Wally. However, he had a strange kind of feeling about this as if he could not stop himself. It went way beyond doing Wally a good turn. It was if it was just meant to be.

His bank was sympathetic but they said he needed a guarantor. That is someone with personal assets who would guarantee Jack's loan so that in the event of default they would repay the loan. Jack left the bank and decided he would ask his Dad who seemed slightly nervous but even so said he would stand him a guarantee of up to £10,000. This meant he did not have to put any money in but just sign on the dotted line.

Within a week, the loan was set up and came through so now he was up and running. He decided to take Wally fully into his confidence on his first day and discussed everything with him so Wally knew that his employment rested on the business creating a good profit. He agreed to pay him 10% above the minimum wage rate with no overtime. This he assured Wally was a temporary arrangement until he saw how things were panning out. Wally seemed totally unperturbed by it and in fact seemed to relish the idea. The first evening he worked until 7pm without complaint, packing up the products in a very cold lockup garage that Jack had been renting for storage. They went out for a beer and Jack spent time filling him in on as much as possible. Wally was silent and Jack hoped that was because he was listening.

He began to realise over the next few weeks the importance of good administration. He started to get in a bit of a mess with all his invoices to customers, who had paid and also who he owed money to. He decided it was now time to see Ashna again and he realised it was little to do with his book-keeping requirements and more to do with seeing her. He felt very confident when he was with her and totally relaxed so he Facebooked her and asked her what she was up to and whether she could give him a lesson on administration. She accepted his friend request which pleased him as she replied within the hour and they agreed to meet at her office at 4PM the next day.

"So what's the problem Jack?"

He told her about taking on Wally and how well he had turned out and also about the loan although he had not asked the bank about its rate at which she became very quiet. Then the administration problem was mentioned and so Ashna put her teaching hat on.

"The first thing is that there are three main books to be aware of – the cash book, the sales ledger and the purchase ledger. A ledger is a book of account to record transactions in and out with a beginning balance and an end balance. Book-keeping systems use what is known as the 'Double Entry' system, which was, interestingly, first documented in the 15th century by a Franciscan Friar called Luca Pacioli. It uses a debit and credit system where a debit is on the left and a credit is on the right. For every debit there is a corresponding credit.

"You mean like Newton's third Law of Motion – 'For every action there is an equal and opposite reaction'. At least I think it was his third" cut in Jack.

"Good analogy. For example, in the depreciation example we looked at before, depreciation is a cost in the Income Statement would be a debit and would be a credit to the Asset account (deducted from the Asset Net Book Value).

- The Cash Book records all of your transactions that pass through the bank. It therefore should show all of your receipts and

payments. It should be a mirror of your bank statements.
is meant that when you put money in your bank it would sho
debit in your cash book but would show as a credit in your l    ...
statement when you receive it. This is because the bank sees it
as a creditor (they owe you as it is your money). I do not know if
that helps or not."

"No, not a bit but carry on anyway" mused Jack.

"O.K. but just remember that a debit is on the left and will either be a
cost in the Income Statement or an Asset in the Balance Sheet. A
credit is on the right and will either be income in the Income Statement
or a Liability (or Capital) in the Balance Sheet. At least that covers 95%
of the transactions."

"Just one thing" cut in Jack. "Why is it called a cash book and not a
bank book. To me cash is dough, moolah, rhino, spondulicks, holding
folding, quid, buck, Oxford, dosh, clams, bread, lucre, paper, green
stuff, Benjamins?"

"Hang on, I haven't heard of Oxfords. Where does that term come
from?" Ashna had her dark eyebrows raised almost off the top of her
head.

"It's Cockney rhyming slang init? Short for Oxford scholar – dollar. So
you would say 'got any Oxfords mate' or 'can I borrow some Jumpin'
Jack Flash' i.e. cash. It comes originally from the East End of London."

"Aha, I see. To an accountant cash means 'instant' money as opposed to
on credit so it is either cash or cheques. By cash in the hand or on the
premises we would call that petty cash. Onto the next book.

- The Sales Ledger records all the invoices sent to customers and
  all the payments received from customers. The balance remaining
  will be what, Jack?"

"What they still owe you. I think you called that the Accounts Receivable (or Debtors)"

"Great job. Yes, if you have invoiced customers £35,000 and they have paid you so far £25,000 then they still owe you £10,000 and this is the Accounts Receivable and would be a debit.

- The Purchase Ledger is similar to the sales ledger except that the entries are the other way around. The invoices received from suppliers are on the credit side and the payments you have made to them are on the debit (left) side. The balance remaining is called Accounts Payable (or Creditors). This is what you still owe them.

I shall show you a picture of how they fit together assuming a starting position of £1,000 in the bank, the Accounts Receivable of £3,000 and Accounts Payable of £1,500.

CASH BOOK          Debits                                    Credits

| Opening Balance | 1,000 | | |
|---|---|---|---|
| Cheques received | 2,600 | Cheques paid out | 5,100 |
| Balance Carried Forward | 1,500 | | |
| Totals | 5,100 | Totals | 5,100 |
| | | Balance Brought Down | 1,500 |

SALES LEDGER

| Opening Balance | 3,000 | | |
|---|---|---|---|
| Invoices to Customers | 5,300 | Cheques received | 2,600 |
| | | Balance carried forward | 5,700 |
| Totals | 8,300 | Totals | 8,300 |
| Balance Brought Down | 5,700 | | |

# PURCHASE LEDGER

|  | Debits |  | Credits |  |
|---|---|---|---|---|
|  |  | Opening Balance | 1,500 |
| Cheques paid out | 5,100 | Invoices from Suppliers | 7,750 |
| Balance carried forward | 4,150 |  |  |
| Totals | 9,250 | Totals | 9,250 |
|  |  | Balance Brought Down | 4,150 |

You can see the double entry here. The cheques received in the cash book (Debits) are £2,600 and these also show as Credits in the sales ledger because money received reduces the amount still left due. Similarly, the Cheques paid out (Debits) of £5,100 on the Purchase Ledger (reducing the amount now owed) show as a Credit in the Cash book as they reduce the bank balance. The result is that in this case the bank has gone from £1,000 in hand to an overdraft of £1,500."

"So what is meant by balance carried forward and brought forward then?"

"The balance carried forward is the difference between the two sides placed in the smaller side to make the two columns equal. The columns will be totalled up every month. The balance brought down is the resulting balance either owed or owing and is the compensating (double) entry for the balance carried forward. All of these balances and subtotals are entered into what is called the Nominal Ledger and from that a 'Trial Balance' is produced. This is a summary of all the account headings in the books and the total debits will equal the total credits. Adjustments are made to some of the balances such as for depreciation, year-end stock and bad debts expected and the resulting balances are used to create the Income Statement and Balance Sheet."

It will look something like this:

| EXTENDED TRIAL BALANCE | Costs and Assets | Income and Liabilities | Adjustments | | Income Statement | | Balance Sheet | |
|---|---|---|---|---|---|---|---|---|
| | Dr | Cr | Dr | Cr | Dr | Cr | Dr | Cr |
| Capital | | 75000 | | | | | | 75000 |
| Drawings | 7000 | | | | | | 7000 | |
| Premises | 100000 | | | | | | 100000 | |
| Fittings | 20000 | | | | | | 20000 | |
| VAT | | 2000 | | | | | | 2000 |
| Loan | | 50000 | | | | | | 50000 |
| Stock | | | 10500 | | | | 10500 | |
| Petty Cash | 50 | | | | | | 50 | |
| A/Cs Receivable | 10500 | | | | | | 10500 | |
| A/Cs Payable | | 14500 | | | | | | 14500 |
| Sales | | 155000 | | | | 155000 | | |
| Purchases | 117500 | | | 10500 | 107000 | | | |
| Wages | 23500 | | | | 23500 | | | |
| Admin Expenses | 5000 | | | | 5000 | | | |
| Telephone | 500 | | | | 500 | | | |
| Rent | 750 | | | | 750 | | | |
| Heat and Light | 1200 | | | | 1200 | | | |
| Travel Expenses | 550 | | | | 550 | | | |
| Interest Payable | 4500 | | | | 4500 | | | |
| Bank Balance | 5450 | | | | | | 5450 | |
| | 296500 | 296500 | 10500 | 10500 | 143000 | 155000 | 153500 | 141500 |
| Profit for Year | | | | | 12000 | | | 12000 |

Notice that the Debit (Dr) column is all costs or assets and the Credit (Cr) column is all income or liabilities or capital. (The Capital can be viewed as a liability in that it is owed back to the owner). Jack was beginning to lose interest here and Ashna could see that so she decided to move on quickly.

"Right, we have covered the 3 main accounting books. I emphasise main because there would also be a book recording the Petty cash Income and Expenditure as well as stock records and your summary book called the Nominal Ledger. These books are usually not in book form these days but recorded on a computer (apart from the Petty Cash) so that the management information is easily summarised and accessed. I would suggest you use Excel to record all your invoices in and out but as you grow you are better using some standard accounting software such as Sage or Quickbooks as these automatically do your double entry and it can be used to work out your budgets and employees' wages as well. Let's just finish off with looking at your sales and purchasing systems."

"Do we have to? It sounds exceedingly boring."

"Let me ask you a question or two? How do you know that you have sent all your customers' invoices for the products they have had? How do you know they have all paid you or how much money is due in this month? How do you know that your goods you think are in the warehouse have not been stolen? How do you know that what you have had delivered to you are what you ordered? How do you know you have been invoiced for what you have received?"

"Ugh. I try to remember it all. I don't really know, I suppose." Jack realised he had a lot to learn to build up a £30 million business.

"Here are some notes I made yesterday about further accounting systems on sales and purchases that you might wish to read." (see appendix Part 1/1) Jack placed them sheepishly in his carrier bag and realised he would have to do some homework. He now wished he had done a business course at university instead of his Maths degree. At least he had learnt about Excel so that was useful.

He swithered about asking Ashna out again but chickened out and as he bade her goodbye he thought he detected a small look of expectancy about her as if she was waiting for him to make a move. He still could not determine whether he would have been lucky or not!

*Further reading in Appendices Part 1/1*

*More practice Questions and Answers on this chapter in Appendices Part 2.*

## Key Chapter Points

- Three main books of account – Cash book (centre of system), Purchase Ledger and Sales Ledger
- Uses Debits (on left) and (Credits on right) – total debits will equal total credits
- Debits are costs or assets, credits are income or liabilities
- Books interconnect by 'double entry' book-keeping system where for every debit there is a corresponding credit
- Monthly summaries are transferred into the Nominal Ledger
- All the balances in the Nominal Ledger go into a Trial Balance which after adjustments forms the basis of the Income Statement and the Balance Sheet

# 7.   Limited Companies

Jack's business grew during the next year as he had increased his product lines to include jeans, printed tee shirts, polo shirts and a few trainers. He did not make much money but he established his channels of distribution, gained good credit with his suppliers and managed to pay Wally a decent wage. He had turned out to be a great success and Jack seriously doubted he could have done nearly as well without him. Wally showed himself to be a good worker who did not watch the clock and one Thursday he came in looking terrible and was obviously sick. Jack sent him home and said not to come back until Monday as he did not want the lurgy, whatever it was. Wally was in at 7am on the Monday and from that moment Jack realised that he had about as trustworthy an employee as he could hope for. Wally's ideas on products were also very astute as he managed to help Jack with translating some of the latest designs into what would be saleable on the high street.

His biggest problem had been his marketing costs. He had set aside £5,000 for a new website and £4,000 for the rental of a small warehouse and office as well as general marketing costs, printing, signs, leaflets & flyers etc. The new website alone had cost him £12,000 as he had decided to go for a good package which included website optimisation and automatic links with Facebook and Twitter. The photography had cost him a bomb as he thought he could do it himself and soon realised what an amateur he was. Anyway he was well on the way and he wanted to see Ashna as he was unsure about whether to convert to a Limited Company or not. In fact he did not really know what it meant. He had met her a couple of times during the year for a coffee at Grinder's Coffee House on the pretext of some spurious question but he really had only wanted to keep in touch. He missed her and the idea of a Limited Company would provide a substantial reason for a meeting. Hopefully a long one.

He Facebooked her suggesting he take her out to lunch at a rather pretentious local restaurant called 'Chez Pierre' which had some great Mediterranean salads and she came back to him within 5 minutes accepting. He would have preferred Roscoe's burger bar as their chips were awesome but he had a hunch that her tastes were a little more refined than that and, boy, did he want to impress her. They met there, as he thought it looked a bit obvious if he picked her up. When she arrived he gazed at her in slack-jawed awe as she wore the best cut pale grey trouser suite he had ever seen and she had shortened her hair to a bob which gave her a jaunty look and the appearance of someone in total control of her life. Her heels, which brought her just about up to his arm pits, completed the look. This was not familiar territory for Jack and he gazed down at his beer stained shoes and felt like a total slob. He had this feeling, but only for a moment, as Jack was a positive fellow and the one thing that had not changed about her was her smile. It put him straight at ease. He felt like he had only seen her yesterday and they fell into the kind of easy conversation you have with your oldest friend. She suggested that they share a Greek style salad with feta cheese and olives etc. and then he was astonished to find that this bit of stuff you could blow off your plate was supposed to be a main course. He ate mountains of crusty bread as surreptitiously as he could to stave off the hunger. She suggested they have a chat before ordering a desert so Jack filled Ashna in on developments and she had a suitably impressed look on her face. He then asked about whether it was worth having a Limited Company.

"At the moment, you are trading as a sole trader which means that the profit you are making is effectively recognised as your income whether you draw a lot or a little. This means that in your case you are paying

40% tax on the higher levels of your profit above £32,011 (after your personal allowances). As a Limited Company, you can conserve more of your profits in the company for growth as the corporation tax rate is approximately 20-23% depending on size but even the higher rate is falling to 20%. There are some key points to outline though which I have listed on this summary here:

1. Firstly, a Limited Company is a separate legal entity – it is a perpetual entity even though shareholders change. The directors manage the company on behalf of the shareholders (owners) who elect the directors. In your case you would be the sole director and also I assume the owner of all the shares. Neither the shareholders nor directors can be taken to court (other than for fraud) as the company itself would be sued as it is a separate entity.

2. The company would be responsible for its own debts (liabilities) and you would no longer be personally liable for them as you are at present. If the company was liquidated due to financial problems and it could not carry on trading, any shortfall in the payments to the creditors would not need to be met by you personally.

3. You would have to form a company and register it online for £20 or so through an agent filing the Memorandum of Association which covers the key items such as name, registered office, capital etc and the Articles of Association which state and how the company will be managed. If the Standard Model Articles are used they would not need to be filed.

4. A Public Limited Company (Plc after its name) can offer its shares for sale to the public whereas a Private Limited Company (Ltd after its name) cannot, as would be the case with your company.

5. The Capital Account looks a little different which we shall look at later

6. It is easier to attract finance because not only is a bank more comfortable lending to a limited company but also new investors are easier to attract because the shareholding is easily divisible i.e. there can be many shares.

7. A Limited company implies more substance and is governed by company law so is more credible in the marketplace. Incidentally, a book on company law is very large and covers the combined Companies Acts drawn up since 1948. The directors are deemed to know it so must take advice as clearly without being lawyers or accountants, they would struggle to know or even understand some of it.

8. A critical number of shares to own is greater than 50% of the Issued shares as that that gives day to day control of decisions. Owning 75% or more gives virtually total control.

"Ok I see. You are trying to baffle me with all the legal jargon and succeeding" groaned Jack "but I am a little unsure about this shareholding business".

"A company is owned by its shareholders. Shares are 'issued' and let us say 300 are issued at £1 each. That means that if I own 151 shares I own more than half of the company. For instance, I own 55,000 shares in The Dredger Oil Co PLC, does that mean I own a lot of it? It might do but in this case The Dredger Oil Co has issued 10,000,000 shares so I own only 0.55% of it. (55,000 ÷10,000,000 X 100). Here is a question for you for Dodgy Dealing Ltd. There are 2,500 Issued Shares. There are 4 directors - Jack has 1,240, Imtiaz has 650, Camilla has 555 and Mo has 55. Has Jack got control and do Mo's shares have much value? Try to answer the question below.

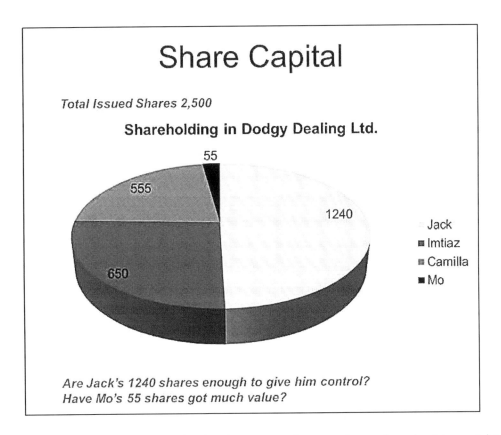

# Share Capital

*Total Issued Shares 2,500*

**Shareholding in Dodgy Dealing Ltd.**

55

555

1240

650

Jack
∎ Imtiaz
∎ Camilla
∎ Mo

*Are Jack's 1240 shares enough to give him control?*
*Have Mo's 55 shares got much value?*

Jack thought about it. He looked up at Ashna and saw her looking at him expectantly. He had better try hard on this one.

"Jack has the most shares so really has the most individual influence. However, to have control he would need more than half of the 2,500 shares which would be 1,250. With 1,240 shares he therefore needs another 11 shares so all the other shareholders could gang up on him and force him off the board of directors. Alternatively, Mo could side with Jack and get a good deal from him in return for his support. In other words, Mo could have a great deal of influence over Jack assuming that the other shareholders were against him. Why is his name Jack anyway?"

"I thought it would help you see the sort of mess you could get in if the company grew and you had other investors. Always keep over half of the issued shares to ensure your position."

"Thanks. Good point. What does being a director of a Limited Company mean?"

"The directors have a fiduciary duty to the company which means they are in a position of trust. For instance, one should declare any conflicts of interest such as being a director of a supplying company and they should maintain appropriate accounting records, publish financial statements and a directors' report and they are guided by rules from:

- International Financial Reporting Standards (IFRS )

- Company Law

- London Stock Exchange (for a Public Quoted Company)

Why do you think these rules are necessary, Jack?"

"I assume it means they are all drawn up with the same rules and therefore it makes them easy to compare."

"Correct and they are hopefully more accurate as well because accounts include many assumptions and it is necessary to ensure directors as far as possible use the same guidelines to make their assumptions. There is also an auditor's report published which provides an opinion by an independent auditor about whether the financial statements provide a true and fair view of the financial health of the business and in a large company the directors' report provides financial and non-financial nature beyond that contained in the financial statements, eg social and environmental reporting. "

"Social and environmental reporting! Is that really necessary?" Jack was aghast at this and longing for his dessert. "What about an ice cream or a banana longboat?" he was almost begging.

"I won't but you go ahead" smiled Ashna.

He ordered a raspberry, chocolate and vanilla mixture which duly arrived in a long thin dish.

"Whilst you are eating your ice cream, we can talk briefly about the social and environmental reporting. Social reporting is about how the company interacts with people. This covers the people working for the company and also those working for its suppliers. For instance, you would wish your employees to be paid a reasonable amount for the job they do and be in good working conditions. Working conditions down a gold mine are a prime example."

Jack had pink ice cream running down his chin from where he had missed his mouth with a very large spoonful. "So why do we care about how suppliers treat their employees?"

"If you are buying from a company that treats its employees very badly, then it could affect where your potential customers go for their products. What if you are buying from a company that uses child labour and your customers hear of this which happened a while ago with one very large sports shoe company? The result could be catastrophic for your image."

"Aha" dribbled Jack between spoonfulls. "I guess the environmental reporting is also about how you conserve resources such as water, oil, recyclable products or reusable packaging or providing for rubbish collection and processing."

"Yes. That is pretty much it, Jack."

The waitress brought the bill just as Jack had filled his mouth with the last remaining blobs of ice cream. The massive size of the bill caused him to inhale very sharply and he quickly realised the error of his ways. He tried to breathe without success and gave one enormous cough which initiated a large ice cream guided missile to launch itself from his mouth straight towards Ashna. From there everything seemed to go into slow motion, seemingly prolonging the pain and embarrassment of the situation. After the smile froze on her face, Ashna's eyes seemed to widen as she realised there was no escaping. The small feeling of relief at being able to breathe did not compensate for Jack's horror of the event. The multi-coloured plug of ice cream hit Ashna square on the point of her chin and slithered quickly down onto her chest and down her formerly immaculate grey jacket ending up in her lap which sadly had no napkin covering it. Around this frozen missile there was further destruction that was something akin to shrapnel from a bomb. There was a chocolate, cream and red spray of ice cream covering Ashna's face and the wall either side of her head. He remembered noticing later the shape of her head outlined on the wall behind where she sat. He would have found it amusing if it had been someone else but now he did not see the funny side. Ashna momentarily did not even blink. She then got up, stunned, and slowly, without a word, left the restaurant gently mopping herself with a napkin supplied by a sympathetic Pierre. Jack removed some notes from his pocket with very sticky fingers to pay the bill and wondered if he would ever see her again. He knew that 'Chez Pierre' would not be seeing him again soon and would probably need a makeover.

When he arrived back at the business, Wally asked him what was wrong and all he could do was grunt something incomprehensible. He got out the smokes but they did not make him feel any better. He went for an early swift one at the pub inviting Wally to join him. He confessed all to Wally who respectfully held back as long as he could but as soon as he heard about the head shaped spray on the wall let out the loudest guffaw Jack had ever heard and suddenly Jack felt better. A couple more glasses of Old Smokey beer and he was at least 80% of his former self and the sight of Wally laughing as they parted actually made him start to see the funny side.

For days, Jack could not bring himself to phone Ashna so he decided to send her a bunch of roses with a little apologetic note. That really did the trick as he had a call from her the next day. He could tell she was laughing all the while she was talking and had clearly forgiven him which was a massive relief to him as he did not want to lose a friend as well as an adviser. She suggested they meet again as there were still some issues to run over related to a Limited company namely, the Capital Account and the Income Statement and they need to get started if he was to continue trading through a Limited Company.

"How about we meet at Grinder's Coffee House this time?" suggested Jack.

"On one condition" said Ashna "that you on no account order ice cream again" and they both laughed.

As usual Ashna was dressed immaculately and Jack had tried to brighten himself up a little by wearing some of his newer lines of jeans and a polo shirt.

"I thought you might have come in overalls this time" joked Jack.

"Jack, please forget about it. My suit was fine after the dry cleaners had given it a good going over. Ice cream is not that bad at staining. So to business. Firstly, the Capital Account. On a non-limited company the profit is calculated and added to the initial capital. Drawings are deducted to arrive at the closing capital as happens at present. OK?"

"Fine by me."

"On a limited company, the profit is arrived at after the directors draw a salary like any other employee and there are no drawings. The capital figure remains always the same (unless new capital is invested) and the profit retained figure grows each year by the profit for that year less any dividends that are paid to shareholders. So we have a comparison as follows:

- Non Limited Company – Capital A/C

|  |  |
|---|---|
| Opening capital | £1,000 |
| Profit for Year | £400 |
|  | £1,400 |
| Drawings | -£250 |
| Closing Capital | £1,150 |

- Limited Company Share Capital

| Share Capital |  | £800 |
|---|---|---|
| Profit to date | £200 |  |
| Profit for Year | £400 |  |
|  | £600 |  |
| Dividend | -£250 |  |
| Retained Profit |  | £350 |
| Shareholders' Funds (Equity Value) |  | £1,150 |

Note that the dividend is a bit like the drawings were before. The retained profit figure keeps moving up (assuming a profit) and this increases the overall Shareholders' Funds, which is the Share Capital plus the retained profit. This is known as Equity Value and the most common shares are known as Ordinary Shares otherwise known as Equities.

"Aaaah" mused Jack "that is why I see the shares listed at the back of papers are called Equities."

"Very good Jack. Dead right." She was increasingly impressed with what Jack was taking in. That was when he was not blowing lumps of ice cream all over her!

This Capital heading is known as the Statement of Changes in Equity in a larger company and would actually be shown like this:

| | Ordinary Share Capital | Retained Profits | Total Equity |
|---|---|---|---|
| As at 1st July 2012 | £800 | £200 | £1,000 |
| Profit for Year | - | £400 | £400 |
| Dividends | - | -£250 | -£250 |
| As at 30th June 2013 | £800 | £350 | £1,150 |

It is a bit complicated but for larger companies it lays out all the capital movements better.

"O.K. What about the Income Statement then?"

"This is very little different. Firstly, the directors' salaries are just another over head like any other wage and they reduce the profit (unlike the drawings in a non-limited company which are deducted after arriving at the profit). Secondly, the profit has several levels. The first level is called Operating Profit which is the Profit but Before Interest and Tax (or PBIT). Then we have the Profit before Tax, then the Profit after Tax and finally Retained Profit which is after Dividends have been deducted although this part is only shown in the Balance Sheet (Statement of Changes in Equity) as above. Here is an example:

| | |
|---|---|
| Sales | £100,000 |
| Less Cost of Sales | -40,000 |
| Gross Profit | 60,000 |
| Less Overheads | -35,000 |
| Operating Profit | 25,000 (PBIT) |
| Less Interest Paid | -6,500 |
| | 18,500 |
| Less Taxation | -4,000 |
| Profit after Tax | 14,500 |
| Dividends | -6,350 (on Balance Sheet) |
| Retained Profit | £8,150 (on Balance Sheet) |

Note that if you receive bank interest because you have money on deposit then it would be added on rather than deducted. PBIT is a good term because it tells you what is coming next i.e. Interest then Tax."

"So why is it calculated before interest then?"

"It is because interest is a function of your capital structure and so the size of your loans. It is not an operating cost but a financing cost. This makes the accounts more comparable at the Operating Profit level" explained Ashna in a very school ma'am like way.

"Why don't you try a couple of exercises then?"

"If you think I am going to do 50 press ups in the middle of Grinder's you are very much mistaken" Jack cut in seriously.

"No, no, no, I didn't mean that type of exercise" and then she caught the naughty grin on Jack's face.

"Right then. Try these two.

What is the Retained Profit and the Equity value from the following figures?

Sales £20,000, Overheads £5,000, Interest Paid to bank £1,500, Taxation £1,000), Cost of Sales £10,000, Dividends paid £5,500, Ordinary Share Capital £1,200, Profit to Date £5,600."

Jack fiddled about on the table whilst Ashna went up to the counter to request another two coffees and when she came back he had produced the following:

Income Statement

| | |
|---|---|
| Sales | £20,000 |
| Less Cost of Sales | -10,000 |
| Gross Profit | 10,000 |
| Less Overheads | -5,000 |
| Operating Profit | 5,000 (PBIT) |
| Less Interest Paid | -1,500 |
| | 3,500 |
| Less Taxation | -1,000 |
| Profit after Tax | £2,500 |

Equity

| | | |
|---|---|---|
| Share Capital | | £1,200 |
| Profit to date | 5,600 | |
| Profit for Year | 2,500 | |
| | 8,100 | |
| Dividend | -5,500 | |
| Retained Profit | | 2,600 |
| Total Capital (Equity Value) | | £3,800 |

"Well done, Jack. You have shown the deductions in the correct order to get to the PBIT and then the other deductions to get to the Profit after Tax. You then show this figure added to the retained profit to date and deducted the dividend to get the new retained profit and this is then added to the Share Capital to arrive at the Equity Value. One more thing. Suppose the company started with 2,500 shares of 50p each. (This is the £1,250 Share Capital). What do you think is the value of a 50 pence share now?"

Jack looked baffled as he had done enough and decided to bury himself in his cappuccino leaving much of the froth dribbling down his half shaved chin.

Ashna took pity on him. "The total value of the company has increased from the original £1,250 to £3,800 (Equity value). If the value of the company is £3,800 now do you see?"

"I guess therefore one share is worth £3,800 ÷ 2,500 = £1.52 per share."

"Exactly, so the share value has gained £1.02 (from 50 pence to £1.52). Of course, this is only the Balance Sheet Value and not necessarily what someone would pay for the company."

"Right. Stuff like reputation, quality of product lines, market share, growth etc. would come into the real value."

"You've got it, Jack. Where did you learn that?"

"Dunno really. Guess I read it. I've tried to catch up all the stuff I would have learnt if I had done a business degree by reading the newspapers. I think we may have covered it briefly before as well."

"Well done. It obviously was not wasted. Time I was off so what do you think. Should we form a Limited Company?"

Jack loved the 'we' in her sentence. It really sounded like she was on his side. "What do you think?"

"It is your decision" said Ashna in true accountant style.

"Let's go for it. Even though the ongoing costs will be a bit more, I am thinking long term so the sooner we get a company up and running, the sooner we establish a bit more credibility and perhaps it will help in financing the growth."

"I shall have an off-the-shelf company for you within the week so we just need to sort the name change to WJFP & Co Ltd., the bank account, shareholders and director out. I assume you will be the sole director and shareholder and where do you wish to have the registered office? It can be at our offices if you wish?"

Jack nodded his assent to each question and then asked "I read somewhere that some companies have a company secretary. Would that be helpful?"

"Jack, for a small company, it is not necessary but is an optional formal position as they should be responsible for administration of company documents amongst other things."

"How about you being the company secretary?" said Jack hopefully. "I would pay you, of course. Should we say £2,000 to begin with?"

"I would love to Jack but how do you know you can afford it?"

"Because if I could not afford it, you would not accept it, would you?"

They both went their separate ways but Jack had a very big grin on his face. He had just secured the watchful services of an exceptionally talented (and attractive) accountant in a formal position. He knew enough about the bank to know that that they would appreciate this.

*More practice Questions and Answers on this chapter in Appendices Part 2.*

## Key Chapter Points

- Company is a separate legal entity
- Limited by shares, owned by shareholders and managed by directors
- Subject to Company Law
- Public Limited Company - PLC or Private Limited Company - Ltd.
- Capital account now becomes Members Equity – Shares plus Reserves
- Shareholders are the owners of a company and they delegate the management of the company to the directors. Directors and shareholders may be the same people and usually are in a small company.
- Dividend is paid to shareholders and is a deduction from reserves (retained profits) and so is shown in the Balance Sheet

# 8.  Interpreting Accounts through Ratios

The business grew even more over the next months and had taken on three more employees. Wally the waiter was proving his value time and again in getting Jack out of some holes that he had dug for himself. There was one time that Jack had been looking at some new 'T' shirts and tank tops from a supplier and had assumed that they were 100% cotton as informed by the supplier. Wally had been with him at the supplier's and Jack was just about to sign for an order of £13,500 value when Wally became a little suspicious when he felt the fabric. He examined the label and realised they were 50% man-made fibre and should have cost 35% less. He duly informed Jack who then politely informed the supplier that his price was incorrect as these were not 100% cotton. The supplier apologised profusely and gave a new price of £8,775 and even 'threw in' a few extra items by way of further apology. This made Jack and Wally very suspicious that the supplier knew all along so they always treated him with suspicion from then on.

Jack had seen Ashna regularly each month during the next year and they had discussions long into the evenings. This was fine in the summer months but during the winter it became hard for both of them. Ashna was becoming essential to Jack's decision-making processes and by the end of the year he had completed a full year as a Limited Company and he visited Ashna's office and she duly provided the figures as follows:

# Income Statement and Balance Sheet for year ended 30/06/2014

| Income Statement | | | | Balance Sheet | | | |
| --- | --- | --- | --- | --- | --- | --- | --- |
| A | B | C | D | E | F | G | |
| Sales | | 240,000 | | ASSETS | | | 3 |
| Less Cost of Sales | | | | Non-Current Assets | | | 4 |
| Opening Inventory | 4,200 | | | Car | 12,000 | | 5 |
| Add Purchases | 147,000 | | | Less Depreciation | (4,000) | 8,000 | 6 |
| | 151,200 | | | Current Assets | | | 7 |
| Less Closing Inventory | (57,200) | | | Inventories | 57,200 | | 8 |
| Cost of Sales | | (94,000) | | Accounts Receivable | 50,300 | | 9 |
| Gross Profit | | 146,000 | | | | 107,500 | 10 |
| Less Expenses | | | | Total Assets | | 115,500 | 11 |
| Indirect Wages | 35,400 | | | | | | 12 |
| Director & Sec Salaries | 25,600 | | | EQUITY & LIABILITIES | | | 13 |
| Depreciation | 4,000 | | | Equity | | | 14 |
| Other overheads | 32,400 | (97,400) | | Share Capital | 10,000 | | 15 |
| Operating Profit (PBIT) | | 48,600 | | Profit in Year | 32,900 | | 16 |
| Less Bank Interest Paid | | (7,200) | | | 42,900 | | 17 |
| Profit Before Tax | | 41,400 | | Dividend | (6,000) | | 18 |
| Corporation Tax Due | | (8,500) | | Equity Value | | 36,900 | 19 |
| Profit After Tax | | 32,900 | | Non Current Liabilities - Loans | | 31,800 | 20 |
| | | | | Current Liabilities | | | 21 |
| | | | | Accounts Payable | 12,000 | | 22 |
| | | | | Corporation Tax Due | 8,500 | | 23 |
| | | | | Bank Overdraft | 26,300 | | 24 |
| | | | | | | 46,800 | 25 |
| | | | | | | | 26 |
| | | | | Total Equity & Liabilities | | 115,500 | 27 |

"So beyond making a profit before tax of £41,400 and having a whacking overdraft, what does it all mean?" asked Jack.

Ashna looked at him straight in the eye which made him melt a little inside. "I have prepared a little summary of how you should review your accounts. Firstly, you should be looking at the key absolute figures from the income statement and their growth such as your sales, gross profit and operating profit. Then do the same with your balance sheet figures (the 5 main headings). This brief analysis will often tell you a great deal. In your case the sales have grown by a large amount from £44,000 to £240,000? Suppose next year your sales rise to £300,000 and your net profit after tax to £45,800. What would the growth be?" She put him on the spot.

"Aha" he almost shrieked. "At last my Maths degree will be helpful. The growth in sales would be £60,000 on £240,000 which is 60,000 ÷ 240,000 x 100 = 25% and the growth in profit would be £4,400 (£45,800 - £41,400) on £41,400 which is 4,400 ÷ 41,400 x 100 = 10.63%."

"Correct, so how would you interpret that?"

Jack sat quietly for about a minute. "The profit has gone up so that is good. However, as the sales have gone up 25%, we might expect the profit to go up by a similar amount so if it has not then the costs must have gone up by more than 25% which is bad."

"Quite right Jack. So we need to look at the figures a bit deeper in a more scientific way and not just the income statement figures but also the balance sheet. We do this by means of calculating ratios and then comparing them with last year's figures to look for improvement, with budgeted figures to see if we have hit targets or with our key competitors or if we cannot get those perhaps industry averages. We could call this an analysis toolkit and in it there are a range of ratios but to begin with I suggest we only examine 9 key ratios to be going on with."

"But I like Maths as you know."

"Fine. But let's start slowly. There are two stages. Firstly we do the calculations and then we examine the results and try to interpret them overall. A more precise approach is to use 'average' Balance Sheet figures by adding the previous year and dividing by two but in practice this is not often done as it does not take into account the fluctuations during the year which is the bigger problem. Never try to draw a conclusion from just one ratio. We should examine the ratios using the three questions. Are we profitable, are we stable (solvent) and are we efficient? There are 3 ratios in each section.

**Profitability Ratios**

1. ROCE – Return on Capital Employed (Operating profit (P.B.I.T) ÷ Capital Employed X 100)

(Derived from both Income Statement and Balance Sheet figures)

This ratio is a good measure of overall business performance. In your case it is calculated as

$48,600 ÷ (36,900 + 31,800) \times 100 = 71\%$

This figure is nicely high but is likely to fall as you will need more capital to develop. You would normally expect to target between 15% and 30%. It all depends on how risky the venture would appear to be as anyone would settle for a lower percentage return if the risk was lower.

2. ROS – Return on Sales (P.B.I.T ÷ Sales X 100)

(Derived from Income Statement figures only)

Your calculation would be

$48,600 ÷ 240,000 \times 100 = 20\%$

A low ratio (<5%) implies a high degree of competitiveness in the marketplace assuming this is not just the result of generally poor performance. A high ROCE does not necessarily mean a high ROS and vice versa. A low ratio could also mean the business is low margin but very high volumes needed to make the required profit. The industry average should confirm this.

3. Gross Profit % (Margin)  (Gross Profit ÷ Sales X  100)
(Derived from Income Statement figures only)

Your calculation would be

146,000 ÷ 240,000 X 100  =  61%

This ratio is often a measure of prices in the buy and sell part of the operation. A stable (or increasing if possible) gross margin is desirable. A drop in this ratio may also be due to a change in the product mix (selling more of the products that have a lower margin) or due to a change in the efficiency of the manufacturing (direct wages increase). Calculating the materials/sales and the direct labour/sales ratios in order to pinpoint principal causes of ratio change may further support this ratio. As a broad principle, this ratio should not alter with modest changes in the volume of output as the costs are largely 'variable' meaning they will rise or fall in line with the sales. There is no benchmark that this should be and would be guided by the industry standard,

**Financial Status (Solvency) Ratios**

(All 3 derived from Balance Sheet figures only)

1. Current ratio  (Current Assets ÷ Current Liabilities) : 1
This ratio should be between 1.4 and 2:1. A high ratio is not a problem except that it may point to inefficient management of stock and debtors. It should always be interpreted alongside the quick ratio.

Your calculation would be

107,500 ÷ 46,800  =  2.3:1

2. Quick Ratio  (Liquid Assets ÷ Current Liabilities) : 1
Liquid Assets (very short term) are usually the Current Assets less Inventories

Your calculation would be

50,300 ÷ 46,800 = 1.1:1

Also often referred to as the 'liquid' ratio or the 'acid test', this is a measure of how well the short-term money, which could go out, is covered by the short-term money coming in. It is more important than the Current Ratio as it concentrates on the much shorter term and should usually be above 1:1. A very low (below 0.6) and falling ratio usually spells imminent disaster. However, industries such as supermarkets can survive with a very low ratio if they have high stock turnover and speedy collection of receivables.

3. Gearing (Loans ÷ Capital X 100)
Your calculation would be

31,800 ÷ (36,900 + 31,800) x 100 = 46%

This is a measure of the long-term solvency and basically answers the question 'What proportion of the capital is borrowed?' Greater than 50% is usually reckoned to be 'highly geared' so you would need to be careful about further borrowing. A common alternative gearing measure is the Debt:Equity ratio which is Loans ÷ Equity Value = 31,800 ÷ 36,900 = 86%. 100% with this measure is 50% with the previous measure. (Only one measure would be used)

**Activity (Efficiency) Ratios**

(All 3 derived from both Income Statement and Balance Sheet figures)

1. Inventory Days (Inventory ÷ Cost of Sales x 365)
For cost of sales, sales may be substituted to give a clearer trend although not technically correct.

Your calculation would be

$57,200 \div 94,000 \times 365 = 222$ days

This represents the number of days of stock carried and in your case it is on the high side. You would expect to carry as low stock (days) as possible within the realms of properly servicing customers. I would hope you could get this down to, say, 3 months inventory or 90 days.

Very often, an alternative ratio is used called inventory turnover and is calculated as Cost of Sales $\div$ Inventory $= 94,000 \div 57,200 = 1.64$ times. With this ratio method you would require as high a figure as possible.

Carrying 91 days inventory would be the same as a turnover of 4 times per year.

2. Accounts Receivable Days (Credit given) (Accounts Receivable $\div$ Sales x 365)

Your calculation would be

$50,300 \div 240,000 \times 365 = 76$ days

This gives the average time taken to collect payments in. An increasing period is often indicative of other problems in the company such as poor credit control, quality or marketing issues. Your ratio of 76 days is outside your 60 general credit period and the question is does this accounts receivable represent your average figure throughout the year. If it does perhaps you are not being tough enough on your customers' payment times. Ideally only the 'credit' sales would be used in the ratio.

3. Accounts Payable Days (Credit taken) (Trade Accounts Payable $\div$ Purchases X 365)

Your calculation would be

$12,000 \div 147,000 \times 365 = 30$ days

This means that you pay your bills on average within a month. Note that only the trade payables are used which excludes the corporation tax due (or any other taxes). Also the purchases should be the credit purchases and exclude any purchases not on credit.

Ideally the time period for this ratio should balance with the accounts receivable ratio. Whilst a long period is good from a cash flow viewpoint it is usually a sign of inabilty to pay on time.

The above three ratios all support and help interpret the Current and Quick ratios and indicate the ability to control working capital.

Your ratios are summarised as follows with the calculations shown linked to the row and column headings in the Income Statement and Balance Sheet figures:

| RATIOS | Measure | Calculation | | |
|---|---|---|---|---|
| **Profitability** | | | | |
| Return on Capital Employed (%) | % | =C16/(G19+G20) | 71 | % |
| Return on Sales (%) | % | =C16/C3 | 20 | % |
| Gross Margin (%) | % | =C10/C3 | 61 | % |
| | | | | |
| **Financial Status** | | | | |
| Current | X:1 | =G10/G25 | 2.3 | |
| Acid Test (Quick Ratio) | X:1 | =(G10-F8)/G25 | 1.1 | |
| Gearing (accountants) % | % | =G20/(G20+G19) | 46 | % |
| | | | | |
| **Activity (Efficiency) Ratios** | | | | |
| Inventory Days | days | =F8/-C9*365 | 222 | |
| Accounts Receivable (Debtors) | days | =F9/C3*365 | 76 | |
| Accounts Payable (Creditors) | days | =F22/B6*365 | 30 | |

Note that some ratios are percentages, some are days and some are proper ratios i.e. something to one.

Your summary shows good profitability, good financial status although the gearing is looking a bit high and not so great on the efficiency as you are carrying too much stock and taking more than twice as long to get your money in as paying it out."

"That summary is great as it means I can trace the source of all the ratios back to the actual figures on the accounts so thanks for that. I owe you one." Jack sat and thought for a while before speaking again.

"I agree my inventory is a bit high but that was a peak time of year. However, I will have difficulty arranging to take longer to pay my bills and getting the money in quicker will not be easy."

"Just think, if you could reduce your inventory and accounts receivable by one quarter, that would wipe out your need for an overdraft.(£57,200 + £50,300) ÷ 4 = £26,875."

Jack quickly realised the sense she was talking. "It would save me bank interest on that money as well! O.K. I shall give it a go this year."

"One last thing, I feel I need to talk briefly about an important Strategic Investor ratio called Earnings per Share (EPS). If we doubled our profits one year but had three times the number of shareholders, each shareholder would be worse off because their EPS had fallen. It is therefore critical for a PLC to be increasing its EPS year on year.

For example:

Earnings (after tax) year 1 - £576,000, year 2 - £823,000

Number of Issued Ordinary Shares year 1 - 2 million Shares, year 2 - 2.6 million Shares

Result:

Year 1 EPS = £576,000 ÷ 2,000,000 = £0.288 or 28.8 pence per share

Year 2 EPS = £700,000 ÷ 2,600,000 = £0.269 or 26.9 pence per share

The EPS has slipped despite a rise in profits and this would cause a theoretical proportional fall in the share price."

"I do not quite see the issue here as the profit has increased substantially?" said Jack scratching his head.

"O.K. Let me put it to you in your terms. Suppose you are making £50,000 p.a. and you have one share and another investor was taken in who would inject money and also have one share, thus giving you one share each. If the profits went up to £80,000, how would you feel?"

"Aaaah, I see. Before the £50,000 was all mine but with the new investor the £80,000 is only half mine as we have one share each so I would only gain £40,000 and be worse off. Silly to take them on then."

"Maybe, maybe not. That is just one year and the next year the profits might increase to £120,000 which they could not have done without the new investment. In which case, your share of the profits would be £60,000."

"I get it. Basically, if I am taking on a new partner, I need to be sure that the long-term increase in profits is enough to justify sharing them. I might be better off loaning the money."

Ashna was delighted with Jack's ability to sum up the key points very simply. "Well done. However, you would need to be sure that the loan interest payable was well covered by the Operating Profit. You would want the interest to be at least 5 or 6 times covered (PBIT ÷ Loan Interest). We have covered a lot this morning Jack, so I think we had better call it a day." She was noticing a rapidly increasing glazed expression spreading across his face so got up to signal the end of their chat. "As you correctly said at the beginning, you made a profit of £41,400 and yet you have an overdraft of £26,300 so we shall talk tomorrow about a third statement that links these two. It is called a Cash Flow Statement or Statement of Cash Flows."

"Do we have to talk about it tomorrow as I am ready to poke myself in the eye with a Duke." Ashna raised an eyebrow quizzically. "Duke of York - Fork" he said.

Ashna sat down again. "Ah, more of that Cockney rhyming slang. Where did you learn it as I assume by your northern accent that you are not from London?"

"Yep. I grew up in a little village called Lower Peover. It is spelt P..E..O..V..E..R so it often rudely called Pee Over rather than Peover. It is just outside Knutsford. Great pub there called The Bells. Anyway, who are you to say I have a northern accent? Yours sounds further north than mine. Let me guess. Bolton?"

"Good guess, Jack. My dad came over from Mumbai, India or Bombay as it was called then and he started working with his cousin to build up an import and distribution business. Along the way he met my mum and they got married and I came along a couple of years later. Lived there ever since. I moved here for this job but I nearly did not come as I got off the train at Crewe station and it has to be one of the most ghastly, depressing stations in the country. I so nearly got on another train back. So tell me how did you come across the Cockney rhyming slang?"

"I had a flat mate at Uni who was from the East End and it took me a whole term to understand anything he was saying."

"You learnt some useful stuff at Uni, didn't you?" smiled Ashna. He did not respond apart from smiling back. At that moment, their eyes met and some sort of coded signal passed between them which neither understood at the time but later they would both remember. They agreed to meet the next day to look at the Statement of Cash Flows although Jack was not really looking forward to it. Well, he was actually but not to talk about accounts!

*More practice Questions and Answers on this chapter in Appendices Part 2.*

## *Key Chapter Points*

- Absolute figures over at least 3 years needed to establish a trend
- Trends in actual figures are important
- Ratios are indicators in groups of Profitability, Financial Status and Activity
- Key ratio is Return on Capital Employed (ROCE)
- Judgment of a company needed across all ratios not just one
- Comparisons with previous years, budgets and other companies
- Comparisons with other companies can be difficult due to accounting policies, size, year-end etc.

# 9.    Statement of Cash Flows

The next day they met in Grinders and he caught his breath when he saw Ashna sitting there with such a serene look on her face. There was something about her which made his chest constrict. He sauntered over to her table and immediately knocked the sugar bowl all over her lap whilst trying to appear nonchalant and cool. Failed again. Why did he have to put on this stupid act? Thankfully a trip to the dry cleaners was not necessary this time and they ordered coffees and Ashna went into teaching mode. She would have made a very good teacher.

"Jack, there is one other important document that needs to be published for more substantial companies with a turnover of greater than £25 million and this is called the Statement of Cash Flows or Cash Flow Statement. It links the Income Statement with the Balance Sheet by reconciling the profit made (on the Income Statement) with the movement in cash at the bank (on the Balance Sheet) by tracking the movements in the other Balance Sheet items. It answers the question that many clients have asked me in the past 'How come you tell me I have made a profit of £135,000 over the year and yet my bank balance has got worse by £15,000?' The general reasons are that the profit made has ended up not as cash but as other assets such as a stock increase or a new machine.

It is designed to show the

- Relationship between profit and cash movement during the period.

- Sources of cash for the business.

- How the cash has been used.

- Material movements in assets and liabilities.

It is produced by:

- Calculating the movements of assets and liabilities between balance sheets.
- Adjusting the profit for non-cash items such as depreciation

The sources and uses of funds are shown as follows:

## Sources of Funds:

- Profit (adjusted).
- Sale of Assets.
- Reduced stock and debtors.
- Increased creditors.
- Share issue.
- Increased loans

The opposites of these show how cash has been used as follows:

## Uses of Funds:

- Loss.
- Purchase of Assets.
- Increased stock and debtors.
- Decreased creditors.
- Share buy-back.
- Decreased loans.

"Ok" said Jack, "I can see that a profit will create cash and that the purchase of assets will use cash but why should increased creditors be a source of finance?"

"This is because you need to view it slightly differently. It is not that more creditors create cash it just means that if your creditors have increased it is because you have not paid them and as a result there is more cash in the bank. It does not necessarily mean you are overdue as your creditors will increase when you expand the business anyway. For instance, suppose you made a profit of £20,000 but your creditors had increased by £5,000 (and all other figures staying the same), your cash would have increased by £25,000. Similarly, if you made a profit of £20,000 but your inventory had gone up by £3,000 your cash would only have increased by £20,000 - £3,000 = £17,000 because £3,000 of your cash had gone into Inventory and out of the bank. Imagine if you were a market trader and you made a profit of £30,000 in the year this could show as an increase of £30,000 in your bank as you could be trading without credit and not buying or selling any assets."

"You mean a bigger bulge under the mattress" said Jack flippantly "assuming the cash was wadges of green stuff being undeclared to HMRC". Ashna nodded with a tired, pained expression.

"All right then. Since you think you have grasped it pretty well try to convert the following information into a Statement of Cash Flows.

From the Income Statement, the Profit for the year is £45,000

### Balance Sheets in £'000s

|                    | Year 1 | Year 2 |
|--------------------|--------|--------|
| Non-Current Assets | 475    | 700    |
| Depreciation       |        | -30    |
|                    | 475    | 670    |
| Inventories        | 100    | 130    |
| Accounts Receivable| 300    | 250    |
| Bank               | 300    | -100   |
|                    | 1175   | 950    |
| Accounts Payable   | 200    | 300    |
| Loans              | 650    | 230    |
| Shares             | 100    | 150    |
| Reserves           | 225    | 270    |
|                    | 1175   | 950    |

"Okay" thought Jack. "First we take the profit of £45,000 and add back the depreciation of £30,000. That makes £75,000. Now we move down the Balance Sheet. The stock has increased by £30,000 so that is a use of funds. The debtors have decreased by £50,000 so that is a source of funds. The bank is the difference at the end. The Creditors have increased by £100,000 so that is a source. The loans have decreased by £420,000 so that is a use. There must have been a Share Issue of £50,000 so that is a source. So what do I do now?"

"You have done well here Jack and it should be arranged as follows:"

| Sources: | |
| --- | --- |
| Profit | 45 |
| Add Depreciation | 30 |
| Adjusted Profit | 75 |
| Reduction in Accounts Receivable | 50 |
| Increase in Accounts Payable | 100 |
| Share Issue | 50 |
| (A) | 275 |
| Uses: | |
| Purchase of Fixed Assets | 225 |
| Increase in Inventories | 30 |
| Loan repayments | 420 |
| (B) | 675 |
| Net Movement in Funds (A-B) | (400) |
| | |
| Movement in Bank (£300 to -£100) | (400) |

"So what does it tell me then?" asked Jack dubiously.

"It just is a way of picking out the key movements. The Company made a profit of £45,000 but the bank went down by £400,000. The reason was primarily because it bought Fixed Assets for £225,000 and repaid loans of £420,000."

"Now have a look at the Statement of Cash Flows below and notice how it is arranged in Published Accounts

|  |  | £M |
|---|---|---|
| ■ **Operating profit for period** |  | **154.0** |
| Add Depreciation |  | 3.0 |
| Change in receivables | (1.0) |  |
| Change in payables | 14.0 |  |
| Change in inventories | (66.0) |  |
| Interest paid | (10.0) |  |
| Tax paid | (40.0) |  |
| ■ **Cash generated by operations** |  | **54.0** |
| Purchase of Non-Current Assets |  | (7.0) |
| ■ **Cash generated by investments** |  | **(7.0)** |
| Repayment of Loans | (4.0) |  |
| Dividends paid | (13.0) |  |
| Increase in share capital | 2.0 |  |
| ■ **Cash generated by financing activities** |  | **(15.0)** |
| ■ **Change in cash over period** |  | **32.0** |
| Opening cash balance at start of period |  | (29.0) |
| Closing cash balance at end of period |  | **3.0** |

"There are three main headings. The operating profit is converted into the Cash Generated by Operations by adjusting it for depreciation and changes in the working capital, and deducting interest paid and tax. The next heading is Cash Generated by Investments which is about the purchase and sale of Non-Current Assets. The final heading is Cash

Generated by Financing Activities which is about the Issue of Shares, Loan movements and dividends paid.

In this situation we can see that the company made a good profit of £154 million but after tax and a large increase in Inventories came down to £54 million. This figure should ideally always be a positive figure and increasing because it basically shows that the company is generating cash from its basic operations. Thereafter we can see they spent £7 million on Non-current assets and repaid some loans, issued some shares (which covered half the loan repayments) and paid a big dividend out. Overall the bank improved by £32 million. They actually call this cash and cash equivalents meaning all the monetary accounts added together."

"Is this information not available just by looking at the Balance Sheet movements though?"

"Yes it is but it is produced to save you working out all the movements in figures yourself. The big point is that we need to see that a business is generating cash as well as profit as otherwise it will ultimately fail."

"Right. I can see the point of it but it will be a while until I hit the £25 million turnover mark."

"Don't forget that even though you do not publish a Statement of Cash Flows some of your suppliers may be above that figure and so will have to publish them. These are well worth looking at as you can quickly see what they have been doing with the business assets and liabilities and it might just give you some useful negotiating information."

Jack decided that if it came to that point he would refer it to Ashna to look at but he realised that he still needed to be able to understand what she told him about it. They finished their coffees and Ashna told him that the Statement of Cash Flows naturally led onto another topic which is from where does all the money needed in a business come? It is not just from shareholders but that could wait for quite some time yet. They agreed to meet in a few weeks to discuss it but Jack knew he would not wait that long before he saw her again. What pretence could he use next time?

_More practice Questions and Answers on this chapter in Appendices Part 2._

_Key Chapter Points_

- Shows how the operating profit relates to the movement in the bank
- Produced by taking the profit and, from balance sheet movements, by adding sources of cash and deducting uses of cash – balance is the movement in the bank
- 3 key headings – Operating Cash Flow, Investment Cash Flow and Financing Cash Flow
- It highlights the key items affecting the cash in the bank over the year
- Only legally necessary to be published with turnover in excess of £25 million

# 10.  Sources of Finance

An opportunity arose soon enough for a visit to Ashna as he had another call from a very strange representative from the Slovenian drug cartel who were still interested in finding someone to do their money laundering in the north of the UK. They had clearly found out that he was now running a successful operation and decided they would try to coax him into working with them.  He decided he would meet them but not before talking with Ashna as he wanted to find out what money laundering was all about.

He called and they met up briefly in Grinders over a couple of Lattes and he explained to her what had gone on in the previous meeting. She was very serious at first, then gasped and after he told of his pretence at lunacy she spilt her coffee all over the table she was laughing so much.

"Why did you not just run off?" she spluttered.

"I did not know where to run to. Don't forget I was in a strange country and they would have found me in a jiffy."

"Seems like they have found you again. It could be dangerous meeting them you know. However, if you want rid of them completely, I know someone in the Police Service who has connections with their undercover Anti Money Laundering Unit."

"That could be helpful but what exactly is money laundering?"

"Put simply, it is a way of putting illegal money into a company to make it appear as legitimate sales. It is often cash such as that received from drug dealing and is put it into a company that does many cash transactions as if it is from real customers to 'hide' the source of the money.  My profession is duty bound to report suspicious transactions in a client's accounting information. The people who do this are extremely dangerous as there are often huge sums involved and they often try to take over legitimate businesses to use them as cover. Did he give you a name by any chance?"

"I think he said he was called Drago or something like that. Also, they did mention they might like to make an investment in my company."

"OK, so how do you wish to proceed, Jack?" Now Ashna had a very worried look on her face.

Jack thought for a while and then decided. "Firstly, I would like you to explain to me what the legitimate sources of finance are. After that, I would like to meet your contact in the police and see if we can remove these people once and for all." Suddenly he could not decide whether he felt like a hero or an idiot. Whichever, he had Ashna's attention and he liked that.

Ashna looked shocked and very uneasy. "Have you any idea what you are getting into? O.k. I shall arrange it but meanwhile I should stall them as best you can. Let's get down to business then.

Finance can be for long term use or short term.

## Long Term Sources

There are three main sources of long term finance. The first is Share Capital - money invested by the shareholders, Loan Capital - money lent to the company by the bank and Retained Profits (reserves) - these are the profits made by the company. These three form the denominator of the formula for ROCE, Return on Capital Employed.

Share Capital is normally just called Ordinary Share Capital. It is the number of shares issued times the issued share price. The shareholders expect a high return as they are the last in line to be paid out."

"Oh, do you mean if the company is liquidised?" Jack was becoming all attentive now until he saw Ashna's face move towards laughter.

"No, no, no." She spluttered between giggles and hiccoughs. "Liquidising is what you do with a Kenwood food processor. The term is 'liquidate.' Liquidation means turning all the Assets into cash in order to pay the bills." Jack looked suitably forlorn and decided to have a sip of his drink before trying to re-establish his credibility.

"So why is it called the stockmarket then if it is a place where shares are traded?"

"In the United Kingdom we call them shares but in the United States shares are called stocks. Hence the 'stockmarket'. So Ordinary Shares are referred to as Common Stock. Just to add to the confusion, stock over here refers to inventory or it might refer to loan stock. In the United States loans are referred to as 'Bonds'. Confusing, isn't it?"

"So how do the Shareholders get a high return because normally the dividend is about 4% of the share price according to the newspapers."

Once again Jack had surprised Ashna. "Yes. This is called the 'dividend yield'. Really they only get a high return when they sell their shares for more than they paid for them. In other words, they get a capital growth. Many companies look for an annual capital growth of about 10% and give a 4% dividend yield making a total of 14% return for the shareholder."

"Yes, I can see why this is regarded as a high return. You only pay the bank 5 or 6% on loans at present. So why are they called Ordinary Shares then?"

"This is to differentiate them from another type of share known as Preference Shares. These shares pay a fixed level of dividend and do not normally share in the profits of the company. In other words, they rarely show any significant improvement in share price. People buy them mainly to gain a larger regular dividend as the dividend has to be paid in full before the Ordinary Shareholders receive theirs. On liquidation, they are also paid in full before the Ordinary shareholders so they are less risky. They do not normally have any influence over the decision making in the company as they do not usually get votes at the shareholders meetings. The 'voting rights' are normally only attached to the Ordinary shareholders. I say normally because these shares are 'designer' shares in that you can design many variables into them and I have attached a little summary of Preference shares (Appendix Part 1/2) if you ever wish to know more about them. It will just cloud the issue at the moment though."

"So what about retained profits? How can these help finance a company that needs money quickly?"

"They cannot. Retained profits are internally generated and are not cash like Shares or loans. Of course, if you make a good profit you might hope that eventually it will turn into cash. Often, the profits just mean a bigger business such as more machinery or buildings.

The other main source of long term finance is loans from a bank or elsewhere."

"What do you mean elsewhere?"

"We shall come to that. Again I have shown the other source of loans (the general public) in the Appendix Part 1/2 summary. However, there are some key aspects to loans that you need to sort out with your banker.

Firstly, the amount you need is important as if you borrow too much you might be paying interest on a loan when you also have money in the bank. Unlike an overdraft you are committed to the loan repayments and interest whereas with an overdraft you only pay interest when you use the facility."

"I was told by a mate that if you are going to borrow, then borrow big because if you go under for £5,000 you will get no respect but if you go under for a few million pounds then you are still a bit of a dude" cut in Jack with a wry smile.

"Not sure about that Jack. Although, when you borrow you need to ensure you borrow enough because it is very hard going back to borrow more if you have miscalculated as the bank really have you over a barrel then.

You need a few other key aspects sorting as follows:

- The time period of loan is important. If it is £50,000 over 10 years that is an average £5,000 per annum to repay. If it is over 5 years then it is £10,000 per annum. You need to ensure your profitability is adequate to afford the higher repayments. This should be in the repayment terms along with the rate of interest payable and they are all open to negotiation. They can be tailored to suit your needs and may be secured on your assets or unsecured loans.
- The bank may require covenants such as access to your year-end financial statements or monthly management accounts or they might wish to ensure restrictions on other lending.

- For a Fixed Asset loan such as to purchase a machine, the period of the loan should match the life of asset.

- It should be noted that an overdraft although more flexible may be called in (meaning asked for immediate repayment) whereas a loan may only be called in early after failure by you to make repayments or the bank has reason to think you cannot make repayments."

Ashna noticed a quizzical look on Jack's face and enquired as to what he was thinking.

"It was that last sentence. You said the bank could only call in a loan after failure to make repayments which I understand but the bank having reason to believe that your repayments are in jeopardy seems a bit woolly. It is just an opinion."

"A good point, Jack. If the bank becomes aware that your company is in trouble they have the right to request the loan be repaid immediately. Effectively, if you are on overdraft, they can freeze the overdraft making it impossible for you to repay the loan thereby causing you to default and allowing them to call it in."

Jack's eyes widened with incredulity. "So what you are saying is that the bank can still call in a loan anytime even if they have agreed to a 5 or 10 year period?"

"I think Jack that you have to assume that the bank will do what is in its own best interest and that there is still some integrity left in the profession. After all, they want to lend to companies as that is how they make their interest so calling in a loan early without good reason would not make commercial sense."

"So, are there any other forms of long term finance as I would not necessarily buy a car with a loan?"

"Two common forms of medium term finance, say over 3-5 years, are either Hire Purchase or Finance Leasing. Hire purchase is basically purchasing on an 'instalment plan' and legal ownership only passes to the Hirer once the last payment has been made. You would pay interest each year. Leasing is much more complex in that you do not own the item but have the right to use it for most of its life. For instance, if you lease a car for 5 years, you have effectively used most of its life and the car would be returned at the end of the lease period. It is often a good idea as it will expand your source of borrowing outside your bank and limit their risk making them a little more comfortable with their lending to you. Both of these forms of finance are shown in the Balance Sheet under the Long term Liabilities heading along with loans. I have given you a summary of these sources of finance in the folder." (see appendix Part 1/3)

"Ugh, more light reading material" thought Jack. "So, we have talked about long term finance, well what about short term finance? I assume the overdraft comes into that."

## Short Term Sources

"Correct Jack but there are other sources besides an overdraft. We have already encountered one which is to reduce your inventory. It effectively releases money to spend on other things if you carry less inventory as well as reducing your bank interest, which is why I was so keen on you trying to reduce it this year. You can also get a short term loan and you will sometimes see short term loans under Current Liabilities in the Balance Sheet. (Appendix Part 1/4)

A big problem for companies is often the cost of finance for the time it takes the customers to pay. In other words, the accounts receivable ratio is too long. It could be as much as 60 days or even 90 days because the customers are also struggling to pay their bills. The company still needs to finance its purchases, wages and other overheads until the customers pay and in an expansion situation this can be a sure way to company destruction."

"Can't we just send in a couple of heavies with baseball bats?" asked Jack but really knowing the answer.

"Apart from the fact that it is not a nice thing to do there is a small matter of the illegality of threatened violence and these may be good customers with whom you want future business" sighed Ashna.

"So we go to the bank then and ask them for more money."

"And the bank will think what? All the things we talked about with the Accounts Receivable ratio. They may think you have a marketing problem (selling to people who cannot pay), a quality problem (providing poor goods that customers will not pay for) or a management problem (inability to manage the credit control process). What we can do is one of two things. We can offer customers a 'settlement discount' to pay quickly (e.g. 2% off if paid within 30 days) or we can sell our Accounts Receivable (Debtors)" she announced.

Jack looked stunned and sat silently with a thoughtful expression for a few moments before he beckoned her to continue.

"Yes we can effectively get someone else called a 'Debt Factor' to collect our debts in return for a fee."

"But that's what I suggested with the baseball bats" laughed Jack as he was on a roll now.

"This is legal although expensive. Essentially what happens is that you go to a Debt Factoring company which is usually owned by a bank and sell them the Accounts Receivables, which let us say is worth £40,000. They will give you, say, 75% of the value (£30,000) immediately and you will instruct your customer to then pay them. They will collect the debt and then after deducting their fees, pass the balance to you. This means that you get plenty of cash to finance your ongoing business, you do not need to chase your customers for money as they will do it but it comes at a cost. It is really only worth doing if your business is growing and you are making adequate margin to cope with the charges which can be significant. They can be as high as 5% of your turnover so if your profit is less than 5% of the turnover it will put you into a loss."

"Unless we do a much greater turnover and so make a higher net profit:sales ratio."

"That's right Jack so it needs looking into very carefully. There is one benefit in that you can save in staff on your credit control. No one needed to be chasing the customer all the time. Look at this picture of the process:

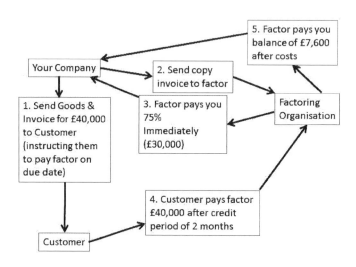

Note that the factor's second payment to you is after the customer pays him and he then deducts the 5% fee of £2,000 (£40,000 x 5%) and the 2 months interest on the £30,000 of £400 (£30,000 x say, 8% ÷ 6). Total costs £2,400. As you can see it is expensive. Another problem is that the customer is aware that you are factoring and this may show a little weakness to your customer. Another method of financing debtors is known as 'Invoice Discounting'. This is where you effectively get an ongoing draw-down facility (like an overdraft) that is equivalent to, say, 75% of your ongoing accounts receivable balance. The customers would pay you directly and not the factor."

"I didn't understand a word of that" grunted Jack.

"Well, let us suppose you are owed £100,000 by your Accounts Receivables. You could get this balance 'discounted' and an agreed percentage, say, 75% paid immediately to you. That would be £75,000. If you then invoice another £20,000 to your customers and your customers have paid you £8,000, that would mean your accounts receivable have increased by £20,000 - £8,000 = £12,000 so you could then draw down an extra 75% of £12,000 = £9,000. Like factoring this works well if you are expanding but not if you are contracting. Your customers will pay you and you need to be a much more stable and substantial company for this method to be granted and the turnover charge will be much lower at perhaps 0.5%. If you want to investigate this you should Google 'Asset Based Lending' and WWW.ABFA.og.uk/public gives some good information on it."

Jack was nearing his limit with this stuff and besides which it did not really interest him too much at present but he could see the point of getting 75-80% of his money paid straightaway as it would help the business grow more quickly without restriction.

"What about just not paying my suppliers" suggested Jack. "Would that not help my cash flow? I guess they would then be after me with a baseball bat."

"Of course that is a good source of finance just like a bank overdraft facility. You are effectively borrowing money off your suppliers. It is obviously best if it is done by negotiation with the suppliers rather than just not paying them on time as that only creates aggravation. Sometimes you can negotiate credit without it costing you if you are offering to give them more business but often they will ask for either a higher price with a settlement discount if you pay early. Remember that if they offer 2% off for you to pay one month early that equates to 2% x 12 months = 24% interest so it is in your interests to pay early."

"What if I have lots of money in the bank then presumably if I have nothing else to do with the money I may as well pay all the suppliers early who offer a worthwhile settlement discount?"

"Yes. However, just because they do not offer a settlement discount does not mean they will not give you one. I once had a client who had £100,000 spare in the bank earning a low deposit rate of interest. I suggested to him to use it to pay his bills early and he said that he did that anyway to all the suppliers who offered a settlement discount. I convinced him to go back to the others and in a half hour he managed to negotiate enough savings out of the settlement discounts he received to cover my consultancy fees for the next 12 months!"

More and more Jack was beginning to understand the wisdom of working closely with Ashna. Not only did she appear to know her stuff but most of the time she explained it to him in ways that he could understand. He did of course hang onto her every word as he knew he had a big crush on her which sadly she did not seem to reciprocate although she appeared to laugh at all of his jokes even the bad ones. That at least was a good sign as nobody else he could think of did unless they were well hammered during a night out clubbing!

"That pretty much covers it Jack and we have more or less finished with what is called Financial Accounting which is primarily concerned with accurate presentation and analysis of historical figures. We now need to move on to Management Accounting which is about creating information with which to manage a company on a day to day basis. This mainly includes costing and budgeting."

"That sounds more my scene," cut in Jack "but now we need to get this other matter sorted before I get kneecapped or something worse."

"Don't joke about it Jack. I shall be in touch within a couple of days but remember to buy as much time as possible."

Off they went on their separate ways with their separate thoughts. Jack was quite excited but Ashna was a little tense as she had a little more idea of what might lie ahead!

## Further reading in Appendices Part 1/2-4

## Key Chapter Points

- Finance can be long, medium (2-5 years) or short term (less than 1 year)
- Main long term sources of finance – Ordinary Shares (Common Stock), Preference Shares (fixed dividend) or Loans (bonds)
- Profit is a source of finance but it takes time to generate
- Medium term sources – Leasing, Hire purchase and debt factoring
- Short term sources – working capital management (Inventory, Accounts receivable and payable) and bank overdraft.
- Loans are a cheaper form of finance than Shares but have added risks.

# 11. Absorption Costing

Jack was at work the next morning and Wally the waiter received a call from Drago, the Slovenian money launderer. It went something like this.

"Allo. Dis is Drago. Is mad Jack there?"

"Hang on mate. Who are you calling mad?" Wally was indignant at his boss being called mad. If anyone was going to call him mad, Wally was going to do it not some monotonic screwball with no manners.

"Just put Jack on the phone unless you want to go for a long walk with no return journey." It was not what he said but the tone of it that bothered Wally. He handed the receiver over to Jack.

"Jack here. May I help you?"

"Allo old friend. Dis is Drago" The blood ran cold in Jack's veins. "I am in zi UK for a while and I would like to meet you. It could be very profitable for you." Jack thought his voice was out of one of his worst nightmares. Deep, monotone, purposeful and confident of always being told yes.

He did his best not to stutter. "I, er, am away for a week but I could meet you after that if you wish. What is your number and I will give you a call." He tried to sound light hearted and in control.

"I vill contact you. Don't be away zi next week." The phone line went dead.

At least he would live for another week! He contacted Ashna about it and she said she was waiting for a call from her contact in the police. Jack arranged for a meeting in her office as he needed to get some advice on how to cost some of his products as he was going to manufacture some simple items such as T-shirts. In fact, he was going to make some T-shirts from various colours of cloth and then print them up with companies' own logos etc. He did not know how to put a price on the products as some of them took a longer time than others.

He went over to see her and she began by explaining the principle of costing.

"Firstly, why do you think you need to know the cost of making a product?"

"Oh, that's easy. To see how much to sell it for as I obviously need to sell it for more than it cost to make."

"Quite so but it is also a bit more than that. Costing helps to do the following:

- It engenders cost consciousness in managers in that if they know a cost is being measured it makes them more careful.
- Make or buy decisions are easier. It tells you whether it is worth making it yourself rather than buying it in.
- It reveals sources of waste by comparing your costing of, say, material with what you actually use.
- It creates data on which to base your selling prices or quotations to customers.

When you are costing a product or service, there are three main elements. There are the materials in the product, the labour time to make the product and all the other costs which we know as overheads such as your wages, the heat and lighting, motor expenses, accountant's fees etc. The materials for a given product can usually be measured pretty accurately and so can the labour time but the difficulty is that you only know approximately what your total overheads are. This means that you need to spread your overheads across all your products. Let's look at a scenario in your business, Jack.

We shall keep it simple and pretend you are just buying and selling the one product of T-shirts. What is the cost of a T-shirt Jack?"

"I buy them in blocks of 50 for £45 so that's £45 ÷ 50 = 90 pence each"

"So then you just put a mark-up on this to get your selling price right? But how do you know the mark-up is enough to cover all your costs?"

"I don't. I just have to sell as many as possible and hope that is enough."

"Right. Last year your cost of sales was £94,000 and you sold them for £240,000. That gave you a margin of £146,000. So you told me your mark-up to sales was 2.55X the cost so a 90 pence T-short would sell for £2.30 is that right?"

"Correct.

"O.K. Now let us suppose it was all T-shirts so that would mean you sold £240,000 ÷ £2.30 = 104,348 T-shirts. You could now allocate all your overheads to these 104,348 T-shirts evenly. Your total overheads were £97,400 which equates to £97,400 ÷ 104,348 = 93.3 pence this would mean your cost per T-shirt would be:

Materials (Cost per T-shirt)     90 pence

Overheads per T-shirt     93.3 pence

Total cost per T-shirt     183.3 pence (Or just over £1.83) but note this would not cover bank interest and taxation.

In other words your £97,400 overheads have been 'absorbed' equally across the 104,348 T- shirts. Hence the term 'absorption costing'. Therefore if the T-shirts were sold at anything above £1.83 each you would be making a profit before interest on your bank loans.

One of the difficulties about this is you are having to project your overheads ahead to get the costs for the 'next' year rather than the past year and you also need to predict how many you might sell.

Suppose your overheads were the same and you therefore budgeted at 93.3 pence per T-shirt, how many of the overheads would you recover if you only sold 100,000 T-shirts instead of the 104,348 you planned?"

"Aha that's easy" said Jack waking himself up. "It would be 93.3 pence X 100,000 = £93,300."

"But your actual total overheads are still going to be £97,400 so you have 'under-absorbed' £97,400 - £93,300 = £4,100. This means you would not only have lost the profit on the shortfall of T-shirt sales but also lost the under recovery of the overheads of £4,100."

"So the costing is really only as accurate as the budget then?" concluded Jack.

"Brilliant Jack. You have picked this up really well." Jack sat up a little straighter after her warm praise. "However, it does need to get a little more complex as this method of allocating overheads where you take the overheads and divide by the absorption base of units sold only works with a single product company. Imagine what would happen if you made overcoats and they cost £50 each in materials would you really only put the same overhead of 93.3 pence on an overcoat as for a T-shirt? What we need is a method of allocating overheads more fairly based on which products cause the most overheads. We still use the same method of

Total Overheads ÷ base but instead of using the budgeted number of units sold as the base we can use two other very common elements as the base. These are direct labour and machine hours.

Let's go back to the basics of terminology as this will help us to understand the concepts and language of costing.

Costs can be split into fixed and variable costs or direct and indirect costs.

Fixed and variable costs are used in the next chapter and relate to marginal costing and fundamentally a fixed cost is one that does not change with activity so if you sell one more unit the cost stays the same such as rent of the premises. A variable cost is one which changes with volume of activity and the most directly variable is materials.

Direct and Indirect costs are concerned more with what we have been talking about so far. A direct cost is one that is 'attributable' or 'traceable' to the product. For instance, materials and labour are the most directly attributable costs in that with each T-shirt you can trace the raw material cost 'directly' to the product. Similarly, you can trace how much time each T-shirt takes to make (if you are manufacturing them). It is very hard to trace how much of the rent should belong to a given product or how much of the boss's time should relate to a product where there may be 100 different products or services supplied. These are known as Indirect costs as they are not traceable to the item of sale.

Your costs could be broken down as follows:

Materials - Direct & Indirect

Labour   - Direct & Indirect

Overhead - Direct & Indirect

If you are manufacturing T-shirts you would have a breakdown as follows:

Direct Materials – Cloth, thread, packaging,

Direct Labour – wages of those sewing, operating the machinery or packing the products

Direct Overhead - Not a common one but if you paid a royalty to a designer this would fall into this category

These above three are known as 'Prime Costs' and are mainly variable costs.

Indirect Materials – consumables such as machine lubricant (variable) or stationery (fixed)

Indirect Labour – quality controllers or tool setters (variable) and salaries of administrative staff (fixed).

Indirect Overheads – rent, rates heat & light etc. which are largely fixed.

The costs would be apportioned in a multi-product company as follows:

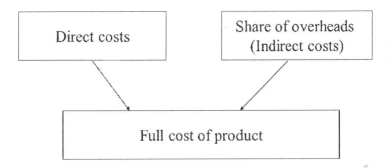

The overheads could be estimated reasonably accurately in total but not easily for each product hence we use different methods of 'absorption' for different situations.

1) A single product company may well allocate the overheads as described by taking:

the projected total overheads (over the period) ÷ number of units planned (over the period)

2) A multi-product company where there is a high volume of labour being used in the manufacturing process may well use:
the projected total overheads (over the period) ÷ number of labour hours planned (over the period)

3) A multi-product company where there is a high value of machinery being used in the manufacturing process may well use:
the projected total overheads (over the period) ÷ number of machine hours planned (over the period)

Each of these calculations would give an overhead 'absorption' rate.

So Jack do you fancy trying a few examples?"

"Very well but a knee-capping by Drago, the Slovenian money launderer is beginning to sound attractive in comparison."

"So question 1 as a recap for a single product company.

You only make one size of T-shirt and each one takes $\frac{1}{2}$ metre of cloth and you buy the cloth as a roll of 50 metres for £80. Your employees are paid £12 per hour and they can make 6 per hour. The overheads for next month are expected to be £12,000 and you anticipate 10,000 sales in the month. What is your cost per unit?"

"Right this seems straightforward. We have materials, labour and overheads.

| | Pence |
|---|---:|
| Materials - Cost per metre is £80 ÷ 50 = 160 pence × ½ metre = | 80 |
| Labour Costs - £12 per hour ÷ 6 / hour = | 200 |
| Prime Costs (Total Direct Costs) = | 280 |
| Overheads - (total overheads ÷ no of units) £12,000 ÷ 10,000 = | 120 |
| Total Costs per unit are therefore | 400 |
| | or £4 each |

"Nothing to teach you is there Jack. Right then question 2. The same situation but this is a multi-product company with the company absorbing overheads based on labour hours. The anticipated labour hours for the next month are 1,200 with all other factors the same."

Jack thought about it for a while. "I assume the materials will not change and neither will the labour costs.

Overhead absorption rate will be £12,000 overheads ÷ 1,200 labour hours = £10 per labour hour. If they do 6 in an hour that is £10 ÷ 6 = £1.67 overheads.

The total costs would therefore be:

| | Pence | |
|---|---:|---|
| Materials | 80 | |
| Labour | 200 | so |
| Prime Costs | 280 | pence as before |
| Overheads | 167 | |
| Total Costs per unit are therefore | 447 | |
| | or £4.47 each" | |

"Last one then Jack. Question 3. Same scenario again but the company recover (absorb) their overheads based on machine hours and they expect to use 500 machine hours next month and they make 16 T shirts per machine hour.

"Once again, the materials will not change and neither will the labour costs.

Overhead absorption rate will be £12,000 overheads ÷ 500 machine hours = £24 per machine hour. If they do 16 per machine hour that is £24 ÷ 16 = £1.50 overheads.

The total costs would therefore be:

|  | Pence |  |
|---|---|---|
| Materials | 80 |  |
| Labour | 200 | so |
| Prime Costs | 280 | as before |
| Overheads | 150 |  |
| Total Costs per unit are therefore | 430 |  |
|  | or £4.30 each |  |

"There you go Jack. Full marks. You have now covered the bones of the Total Absorption Costing technique. A company will pick an overhead recovery method whether per unit or per labour hour or per machine hour. You will also sometimes find that if there are two manufacturing departments where one is very capital intensive with expensive machinery it will use machine hours to recover the overheads. If the other department is basically assembly and therefore labour intensive it will use labour hours instead.

We are really saying that we use only one rate to recover or 'drive' the overheads in each department. In reality there may be several drivers. For instance, design costs (designers' time) may be driven by design complexity such as number of components in the product. Machine setup time may be driven by the number of production runs or products in a run. Advertising may be driven by the number of different designs and so on. When we incorporate all these different 'cost drivers' it is called Activity Based Costing which is appropriate where there are comparatively high overheads. (This is briefly addressed in the Appendices)."

"I can go along with that" interrupted Jack quickly as he had more than enough down this line "but what happens if there are two or more departments, surely each one will have separate overheads as they might be quite distinct. For instance, I have a packing area, a warehousing area and soon I will have a manufacturing area, what would we do then?" He was proud of himself now as he thought he had caught her out.

"That is quite straightforward. We just have to allocate all the costs to their respective areas. Let us just say we have two areas of manufacturing and assembly and total overheads to be shared between the two of £120,000.

The budgeted overheads for the year are made up as follows:

| | |
|---|---|
| Manufacturing consumables | 6,000 |
| Assembly consumables | 2,000 |
| Supervisory wages | 30,000 |
| Canteen costs | 15,000 |
| Rent Costs | 45,000 |
| Machinery Maintenance | 10,000 |
| Heating & Lighting | 12,000 |
| Total Overheads | £120,000 |

You also have the following departmental information:

|  | Manufacturing | Assembly | Totals |
|---|---|---|---|
| Number of Staff | 20 | 20 | 40 |
| Value of Machinery | £60,000 | £20,000 | £80,000 |
| Area occupied | 1,000 m$^2$ | 500 m$^2$ | 1,500 m$^2$ |

So how do you think you would allocate each cost, Jack?"

"Manufacturing and Assembly consumables have got me. Don't know."

"These are materials used 'directly' by the departments such as machine lubricant or cleaning materials" smiled Ashna.

"Ah, so they would be allocated direct to the department then?" pronounced Jack hopefully. Ashna nodded.

"Supervisory wages could be allocated again directly but if the supervisors have general duties then I guess in proportion to the staff in the department. Canteen costs again related to the staff numbers. Rent would have to be in proportion to area. Machinery maintenance would be in proportion to machine value. Heat and light in proportion to area but I guess there is an argument that they are allocated in proportion to staff numbers."

"That's about right. There sometimes is not a clear cut method for each overhead. Now to allocate you would just use the basis of allocation of say the staff numbers and multiply the total overhead cost by the staff numbers in that department and divide by the total staff numbers. So manufacturing has 20 staff out of a total of 40 which is 50% so they would have $\frac{1}{2}$ of the total. The area is 1,000 m$^2$ in manufacturing which is $^2/_3$ of the total so they would have $^2/_3$ of the overheads. The machine value for manufacturing is £60,000 out of a total of £80,000 which is 75% so they would bear $\frac{3}{4}$ of the total overhead with assembly bearing the other 25%.

The overall allocation would look as follows:

| | Method | Totals | Manufacturing | Assembly |
|---|---|---|---|---|
| Manufacturing consumables | Direct | 6,000 | 6,000 | |
| Assembly consumables | Direct | 2,000 | | 2,000 |
| Supervisory wages | Staff Numbers | 30,000 | 15,000 | 15,000 |
| Canteen costs | Staff Nos | 15,000 | 7,500 | 7,500 |
| Rent Costs | Area | 45,000 | 30,000 | 15,000 |
| Machinery Maintenance | Machine Value | 10,000 | 7,500 | 2,500 |
| Heating & Lighting | Area | 12,000 | 8,000 | 4,000 |
| Total Overheads | | £120,000 | £74,000 | £46,000 |

This would mean that Manufacturing would have to recover or absorb £74,000 and Assembly would have to recover £46,000 so each department would have an absorption rate based on these. So if Manufacturing recovered its overheads based on machine hours and its budgeted machine hours for the year were 6,250 and Assembly recovered its overheads based on labour hours and its budgeted labour hours for the year were 5,000, what would be the absorption rates for each department?" Once again she was keeping him occupied. A real slave driver.

"Well, the absorption rate is the Overheads ÷ Base so for the Manufacturing it would be:

£74,000 ÷ 6,250 machine hours = £11.84 per machine hour

and for Assembly it would be:

£46,000 ÷ 5,000 = £9.20 per labour hour."

"Good. Finally, let us apply this further and suppose a job was done in the company with a material cost of £147 with machine time of 7 hours and labour time of 8 hours and the labour is paid £14 per hour this is how we arrive at the total cost?"

| | |
|---|---:|
| Material costs | £147.00 |
| Labour Costs (8 labour hours × £14/hour) | 112.00 |
| Prime Costs | 259.00 |
| Manufacturing Overheads (7 machine hrs × £11.84/machine hour) | 82.88 |
| Assembly Overheads (8 labour hrs × £9.20/labour hour) | 73.60 |
| Total Cost of product | £415.48 |

It was a massive relief that Ashna had actually worked it out for him this time. Suddenly, he felt the deep stirrings in his heart for her again and when he caught her eye he just could not think straight. It was time that he made his move and he decided to plan his strategy carefully as a big rebuff at this stage would dent his confidence. He thought about inviting her to a football match but quickly dismissed that one as he felt it was a less than a 1 in 4 chance that she liked football. Mind you, if she hated football and still came with him he would know he was in with a good chance. High risk strategy that one, so much more thought needed. He decided to leave it until he had sorted things out with the Drago and his henchmen. He stood up and made to leave her office and she held out her hand. It felt very warm and soft as he shook it. He carried on shaking it until she made to retrieve what was left of her hand and he suddenly felt all stupid again. It was years since he had been an awkward student and he always felt a little awkward around Ashna. He just couldn't hack it. He left with a quiet goodbye before he did something even more ridiculous. She agreed to let him know the minute she heard from her police contact.

*More practice Questions and Answers on this chapter in Appendices Part 2.*

## Key Chapter Points

- Costing is not a precise procedure.

- Materials and labour costs may be precise but the allocation of overheads to a product is somewhat arbitrary.

- Costs are broken down and allocated to cost centres and each of these cost centres is monitored and controlled.

- There are a variety of bases which can be used to recover or absorb costs. These create overhead absorption rates (total overheads ÷ budgeted base)

- The accuracy of the costings is totally reliant on the ability to predict future activity levels.

A development of absorption costing is 'activity based costing' (ABC) which recognises that different costs have different cost drivers and so cannot be accurately costed using a single base for absorption.

# 12. Marginal Costing & Decision-Making

Sure enough the next afternoon, Ashna phoned and she had heard from her friend in the police who had told her to text a particular mobile number with one word 'Dufforgans'. Strange word he thought. He sent the text whilst they were on the landline and within seconds he had a reply text saying "Meet back of old cinema in Hasni Street tonight at 1.30 a.m. DO NOT BE LATE. Code word Dufforgans – response is 'Of course they are'. You might be followed."

"Phew. This is getting exciting" he said confidently to Ashna without feeling it. She was very quiet and clearly more than a little worried. "It's only a meeting what harm can it be? Meanwhile I need some more help in deciding which product lines I wish to keep as I was going to drop one or two but Wally said I should not drop any if they make a contribution and I do not know what he is talking about. He also asked me what our break-even is and I had to tell him that I had not a clue."

"Do you know what break-even means, Jack?"

"I would guess it means when I am neither making a profit nor a loss. I am just breaking even."

"Pretty much right. Let's meet up this evening and run through it to take our mind off the other issues. Any suggestions where?"

Jack could not believe his luck. This was the opening he needed and all thanks to Drago. He must remember to thank him if he was allowed to live long enough. "Why don't we go to the new Thai restaurant called Thai Food Tee in Grosvenor Street as I hear it is very good? Suppose I pick you up at around eight." What had happened to him? He was not a take charge kind of guy at all and suddenly he had almost given her instructions.

"That would be marvellous" she replied and she actually sounded to Jack as if she meant it. Even after the last time! They finished the call. 'Don't blow it Jack' was all that went through his mind for the next few hours.

Jack was beside himself at 7.30 as he could not wait for 8 to arrive. He had a shower earlier and then followed it with a bath and threw about a litre of Aramis on. It was expensive he knew but his Dad always said if you are going to smell of anything smell of something good. Wise words. He still had his old banger of a SAAB and he had cleaned it out earlier of parking tickets, old coke cans, fish and chip paper, copper coins, matches and he even found a tenner under one seat which lifted his spirits a little. He almost threw a load of Aramis in the car as well and then realised he did not really wish to smell like the car so just settled for some fly spray as that smelt better than the car.

The SAAB had been repaired after its previous altercation with Merc man although the go faster stripe was still a little off line. But, hey you cannot have everything in life. He was feeling very cheerful.

He picked up Ashna from her home this time as she had given him the address which was another step forward and off they went to Thai Food Tee. Once again she looked amazing and he was struggling to concentrate on the road. Just once he would like to see her looking scruffy but he did not know why.

Sitting down reading the menus they ordered a bottle of light white wine and settled in for the session by candlelight. Jack reiterated about Wally and his break-even conversation. Ashna said best to start with the basics.

"When we talked before about costs related to absorption costing we split the costs into direct and indirect. Effectively, the direct costs are those above the gross profit line and the 'overheads' are the indirect costs. When we apply this to a product, the direct costs of a product (or service) are principally the materials and the labour of the people who make the product (or supply the service). The indirect costs are all the other costs which need to be apportioned across (or absorbed by) all the products. We then arrive at an estimate for the total cost of a given product.

We now need to address a different form of costing called marginal costing so let's work through the following notes I have prepared for you. Incidentally, these techniques are often known as 'costing for decision-making' because they do not give a total cost estimate like absorption costing but help with making certain decisions.

Costs are classified into two main headings when assessing cost behaviour. A *fixed cost* remains unchanged within given output parameters. A *variable cost* varies in significant sympathy with changes in the level of activity. It can vary proportionately to sales or production. What we are really saying here is that a fixed cost is not totally fixed, it simply means that if we make more of the product the cost will not change. Each year rent and rates may change but it is still a fixed cost within this definition.

It is sometimes quite difficult to separate the fixed and variable costs and some costs are known as semi-variable in that they have one element of each. For instance, a salesperson's salary might be paid partly as a basic (fixed cost) and partly as a commission on sales (variable). Similarly, a telephone bill might contain a monthly rental (fixed cost) and a per call charge (variable cost). Have a go later at some of the exercises here (Chapter questions & answers) to see if you can determine which is fixed, variable or semi-variable.

Contribution is the key term in marginal costing and is defined as 'the difference between the sales value and the variable costs' of the product. We say that a product is providing a 'contribution' if this figure is positive.

An Income Statement may be drawn up for a company and then converted into a 'contribution' statement format.

e.g.

| | |
|---|---|
| Sales | £1,000 |
| Less Total costs | 900 |
| Profit | £100 |

Contribution Statement

| | |
|---|---|
| Sales | £1,000 |
| Less Variable Costs | 400 |
| Contribution | 600 |
| Less Fixed Costs | 500 |
| Profit | £100 |

So what would be the break-even (no profit or loss) for the company?"

Jack thought about this. "Instinctively, I look at the total costs of £900 and so if sales are £900 then it is break-even. However, if the sales fall to £900 obviously, the fixed costs will not change because they are fixed. The variable costs, however, will fall in proportion to the sales."

"Dead right, Jack. This 'direct proportion' is one of the fundamental assumptions we make in utilising the marginal costing concept. As can be seen the variable costs are 40% of the sales. (£400)

Therefore, if the sales fall to £900 the variable costs fall to 40% of £900 = £360

We would therefore be left with the following contribution statement:

| Sales | £900 |
|---|---|
| Less Variable Costs | 360 |
| Contribution | 540 |
| Less Fixed Costs | 500 |
| Profit | £40 |

The break-even contribution statement would look as follows:

| Sales | | £833 |
|---|---|---|
| Less Variable Costs | 40% | 333 |
| Contribution | 60% | 500 |
| Less Fixed Costs | | 500 |
| Profit | | £0 |

It can now be seen that if the variable costs are 40% of sales, the contribution is 60% because it is the difference between sales and variable costs. Similarly, if the variable costs were 72%, the contribution would have been 28%, and so on.

The break-even sales figure can be calculated by dividing the fixed costs by the contribution percentage.

So Break-Even = 500 ÷ 60% = £833.

Remember that contribution must equal fixed costs at break-even.

As fixed costs are already assumed to be committed for i.e. sunk , they may be ignored for the purpose of making many decisions. If contribution is maximised this will automatically maximise profit as fixed costs are fixed!

To use marginal costing effectively requires an understanding of the basic assumptions underlying the concept. These are :-

a) Variable costs and therefore contribution are assumed to vary directly proportionately to the activity level (sales or production). Obviously, if sales units are the same as produced units then it has the same effect. In reality, variable costs will not vary directly. For instance, material cost is usually less per item on large orders as there is less wastage and price discounts are more easily negotiated. Similarly, labour costs usually fall due to the experience of the workforce. This is known as the 'experience' or 'learning' curve.

b) Fixed costs remain fixed. In reality, there are jumps in fixed costs with each stage of expansion.

c) Other than a change in product mix, it is only the buying prices and labour rates or selling prices which affect the variable cost %. Higher buying prices result in lower contribution %. Higher selling prices result in higher contribution %.

Have a look at this problem Jack.

| Units Sold | 1200 | @ £20 each |
|---|---|---|
| Sales | | £24,000 |
| Less Variable Costs | 25% | 6,000 |
| Contribution | 75% | £18,000 |
| Less Fixed Costs | | £12,000 |
| Profit | | £6,000 |

What do you think would be the break-even sales figure and how many units?"

"O.k. Working from the profit upwards, the break even means the profit is zero so the contribution would have to be equal to the fixed costs (£12,000) to achieve this. The contribution is 75% of the sales so the sales would have to be the contribution divided by 75% = £12,000 ÷

75% = £16,000 so our new break-even contribution statement would look as follows:

| Units Sold | | 1200 @ £20 each |
|---|---|---|
| Sales | | £16,000 |
| Less Variable Costs | 25% | 4,000 |
| Contribution | 75% | 12,000 |
| Less Fixed Costs | | £12,000 |
| Profit | | 0 |

If the sales are £16,000 and these are sold at £20 each, the break-even units would be £16,000 ÷ £20 = 800 units."

"Jack that is fine. There is a short cut to the break-even in units.

Whereas the break-even level of output in value is the (fixed costs / contribution %).

Now the break-even level of output in units is (fixed costs / contribution per unit)

In the example above break-even is £12,000 ÷ 75% = £16,000 sales.

If we now calculate the contribution on one unit we have Selling Price of £20 less variable costs of £5 (25%) giving us a contribution/unit of £15 (75%)

Break-even is therefore £12,000 ÷ £15 = 800 units.

Try this one Jack. What would the profit be if the sales were budgeted at 1,000 units?"

"Easy one for Mensa kid here. Working down from top to bottom.

| Sales (1,000 @ £20) | | £20,000 |
|---|---|---|
| Less Variable Costs | 25% | 5,000 |
| Contribution | 75% | 15,000 |
| Less Fixed Costs | | 12,000 |
| Profit | | £3,000 |

So the profit would be £3,000"

"Right Jack. Now we can look at one more technique called margin of safety. In this case we expect (or budget) sales of £20,000 and our break-even sales are £16,000. We can therefore say our margin of safety is £4,000. It is the amount by which our budgeted (or actual) sales exceed our break-even sales. It is usually expressed as a percentage of the budgeted sales. So we have the following formula for margin of safety:

(Budgeted Sales less Break-even sales) ÷ Budgeted Sales X 100

(£20,000 - £16,000) ÷ £20,000 X 100 = 20%

This means that the sales can fall 20% from their budget before making a loss. Ideally this percentage would be as high as possible meaning less risk of attaining a loss. Try this one Jack.

Which is the least risky?

| | Expected sales | Break-even Sales |
|---|---|---|
| Situation 1 | £48,000 | £36,000 |
| Situation 2 | £12,000 | £10,000 |

"For Situation 1 the Margin of Safety is

(£48,000 - £36,000) ÷ £48,000 X 100 = 25%

For Situation 2 the Margin of Safety is

(£12,000 - £10,000) ÷ £12,000 X 100 = 16.7%

So Situation 2 would be more risky as it is a smaller percentage fall before making a loss. However, does that depend on the likelihood of Situation 2 falling compared to the likelihood of Situation 1?"

"Very good Jack. I nearly forgot you did a Maths degree. Yes, probability does come into it in the real world but assuming equal probabilities of a fall then Situation 1 would be the least risky."

"Aha" Jack grunted as the first course arrived. He had the Crispy Coriander beef and Ashna had the Battered Aubergines with Penang sauce. The smell was tremendous and it was all Jack could do to stop himself wolfing it down in three mouthfuls as he was so hungry. He had been too excited to eat at lunchtime so he had a big hole to fill. Neither of them spoke whilst they were eating. It was a comfortable silence as they were both hungry and happy in each other's company. At one point, whilst his face was almost buried in his plate his eyes flicked up and he noticed Ashna looking at him with such a soft expression and immediately she turned back to her food slightly embarrassed.

When they had completed their starter, Jack wished he could have licked the plate it tasted so good. Maybe it was the company! He beckoned Ashna to continue with the lesson.

"Are you up for it then Jack?"

"What?" Jack thought all his birthdays had come at once.

"Continuing as you indicated, of course." Ashna suddenly realised that her words could have been taken in a more provocative way and she started to giggle. It was infectious and Jack could not prevent himself laughing as well  and within thirty seconds all the restaurant within earshot were laughing also when they saw these two 'opposites' beginning to cry with laughter. When Jack looked back on that moment he realised it was a significant point in their relationship.

"To business then. Cost behaviour can be shown in a chart known as a break-even chart as shown in the notes (appendix Part 1/5) and is a good way to demonstrate what we have covered in chart form.

Knowing your break-even is a very important aspect of business and working out your overall contribution, contribution % and contribution per unit are fundamental to this. Now we come to an even more exciting aspect of this technique which is known as contribution analysis. We have already decided that as fixed costs are fixed, if we maximise contribution, we shall also maximise profit so now let us look at a scenario for you with 3 product groups:

|  | Totals | T-Shirts | Jumpers | Jeans |
|---|---|---|---|---|
| Sales | £56,000 | 20,000 | 25,000 | 11,000 |
| Variable Costs | 26,000 | 11,000 | 9,000 | 6,000 |
| Contribution | 30,000 | 9,000 | 16,000 | 5,000 |
| Fixed Costs | 25,000 | 7,000 | 10,000 | 8,000 |
| Profit | £5,000 | 2,000 | 6,000 | (3,000) |

What do you think you should do in this situation, Jack?"

"Ha. Fairly straight forward this one. Just drop the Jeans group as it is making a loss."

"Wrong! Blown that Mensa kid." Ashna was really enjoying this and the wine had made her quite rudely familiar with Jack. "You see although the Jeans are making a loss, if they were dropped then there would still be £8,000 of fixed costs to be covered by the other products. The other products are making £8,000 total profit so with added fixed costs of £8,000 overall it would create a break-even situation. The

Jeans are making a £5,000 contribution and in simple terms, which are obviously the terms you need it explaining in Jack, whilst a product is making a positive contribution it should not be dropped."

"I note your derogatory tones, Ash, you seem to have scored one over me."

"Who told you to call me Ash? Actually, I quite like it from you. There are times you might drop a loss making product even though it is making a contribution. Firstly, if you drop your Jeans...." She suddenly realised what she had said and both of them erupted in laughter again just when the main course was being brought to the table. Jack threw his head back with a huge below and sent both the waiter and the plate of King Prawn Stir Fry thick noodles flying through the air. Most of the noodles landed with a heavy 'splat' in the middle of a table of six who, prior to that moment, had been laughing at Jack and Ashna. They weren't laughing now. A single King Prawn had landed and stuck, bolt upright, in one of the ladies' hair. Her eyes went up as if she could see it and then she began cry. Oh dear another meal that Jack had ruined. Jack looked forlorn but Ashna looked at him and then nearly fell off her chair clutching her stomach she was laughing so much. She calmed down and the staff were amazing with cleaning things up, pacifying prawn-hair lady and managing to get another main course for Jack. Ashna had the Chicken in a Hot Thick Red Curry sauce. They again giggled conspiratorially at the thought of that plateful landing in prawn lady's hair.

"So where were we? Ah yes, dropping the Jeans product. If this product was dropped you would lose its contribution of £5,000 so it would need to be replaced. It might be worth dropping if you could also save at least £5,000 on the fixed costs. For instance, the fixed cost of £8,000 might include £5,800 of costs specific to the Jeans production e.g. if they were made in a dedicated factory it might be closed saving all the fixed costs. Alternatively, by dropping the Jeans line, customers might buy more of the other products (doubtful in this case). In fact stopping the Jeans might make the other product sales fall. Also, it may be the Jeans could be replaced by a new product of, say, coats which would create a greater contribution than £5,000. In other words there are product line decisions that can only be made by using this marginal cost technique."

"Aaaallrightyyyy. What other decisions could you use it for?"

"The key aspect is what gives the greatest contribution if there are a series of options. Besides the product line decisions, there are three other main decisions for which this technique can be used:

- Do we buy in the product or make it ourselves?
- Do we accept a special order from a customer at a price that is less than the usual?
- How do we make a product line decision when there is a scarce resource involved?

Let us try a simple example on each one.

## Make or buy in

Suppose we have a product with the following costs if we make the product ourselves:

| | |
|---|---|
| Direct Materials | £45 |
| Direct Labour | £10 |
| Fixed Overheads | £15 |
| Total Costs | £70 |
| Selling Price | £80 |

We can outsource the product and get it made for £60 so should we do that?"

Jack knew there was a catch here but he was not sure what it was. It seemed too simple.

"Our current cost of making it is £70 but if we buy it in for £60 then we shall make £10 more profit so it looks as if it should be bought in but it cannot be that obvious."

"Correct. It is not that obvious Jack. If we buy it in for £60 what costs have we replaced? Clearly we do not have the materials and labour costs of £55 because these are variable costs but what about the Fixed Overheads?" A little glimmer of light showed in Jack's eyes. "The Fixed Overheads will still be there so the overall costs if we buy the product in would be the buying-in costs of £60 plus the Fixed Overheads of £15 making a total cost of £75. So we would be worse off but this assumes that the Fixed Overheads could not be effectively 'used' by another area of the business or reduced. Also, there are other commercial issues such as control over delivery and quality aspects to consider. The basic calculation when buying in is that the cost of buying-in needs to be less than the **Variable** costs of manufacture not just the total costs of manufacture otherwise it is not worth doing.

Accepting a special order

This situation is arises typically where a customer will suggest paying a lower than normal price for the product.

Let us take the previous situation.

| | |
|---|---|
| Direct Materials | £45 |
| Direct Labour | £10 |
| Fixed Overheads | £15 |
| Total Costs | £70 |
| Selling Price | £80 |

At the moment we are making £10 profit per item but suppose the customer said they will place a large order with you but only pay £60 what would you say to that Jack?"

Jack had been caught out once but not again. "I guess the key point is whether we will make a contribution from the order.

If we arrange the costing information to reflect the marginal cost we have:

| | |
|---|---|
| Direct Materials | £45 |
| Direct Labour | £10 |
| Variable Costs | £55 |

Therefore if the customer is paying £60 that will give us £5 (£60 - £55) contribution on each one so that we would be better off by accepting the order."

"Got it in one Jack. Any price above the variable costs will give a contribution and is therefore potentially acceptable. That is what contribution means – a contribution towards covering the fixed costs and the profit."

"What do you mean by potentially acceptable?"

"There are again commercial aspects to consider as although mathematically it would be advantageous to accept the order, it still might not make enough contribution to cover the other risks. Any suggestions Jack?"

"Well, there is a risk with any order such as getting paid for one thing so if the contribution was so low, say only 20 pence per unit, then it is just not worth the effort. Secondly, it might prevent you accepting a better order at full price later on as all the capacity is used up. Thirdly, if you do a very good deal to one customer, then other customers will be dead upset if they found out about it. It could blow the whole goodwill of the company." Jack was enjoying this as it was directly relevant to many decisions he had to make regularly.

"That's good Jack. There is one more decision to look at now.

Limiting Factor

Suppose you have three products to sell next month. Let us say T-shirts, Jumpers and Jeans and you manufacture them with prices and variable costs as follows:

|  | T-Shirts | Jumpers | Jeans |
|---|---|---|---|
| Sales Price/unit | £8 | £25 | £40 |
| Variable Costs | £4 | £10 | £20 |

You are also short of labour time to make the products and the labour hours for each one are as follows:

T-shirts    0.1 hrs

Jumpers    0.75 hrs

Jeans      2.00 hrs

You need to decide how many of each you make up to the product's market potential. What do you reckon Jack?"

"The Jeans obviously make us the most money as follows:

|                   | T-Shirts | Jumpers | Jeans |
|-------------------|----------|---------|-------|
| Sales Price/unit  | £8       | £25     | £40   |
| Variable Costs    | £4       | £10     | £20   |
| Contribution/unit | £4       | £15     | £20   |

and the T-shirts make the least so I would want to sell mostly the Jeans first followed by Jumpers and lastly T-shirts although the volumes of each are obviously important."

"Good Jack but now with a limit on the labour hours we need to sell the most of the products not with the highest contribution but with the highest contribution per labour hour. So we arrange it like this:

|                   | T-Shirts | Jumpers | Jeans |
|-------------------|----------|---------|-------|
| Contribution/unit | £4       | £15     | £20   |
| Labour hours/unit | 0.1      | 0.75    | 2     |
| Contrib/labour hr | £40      | £20     | £10   |
| Priority          | 1        | 2       | 3     |

We use this calculation solely to determine the priority of manufacture and now you can see that we should concentrate on the T-shirts as they make us £40 per labour hour and the Jeans make us the least at £10 per labour hour."

"But surely it is up to the customers what they buy."

"Yes it is but it means you could gear your promotions (and sales staff incentives) towards the T-shirts for that period where you have a limiting factor or scarce resource as it is sometimes called.

Other scarce resources might be square metres of selling space, machine hours or ounces of raw material."

Jack was impressed with this type of calculation as he could see how it could make him more efficient. He knew some orders would take up a huge amount of his time so he thought he could use this calculation technique on these orders to work out the contribution per hour of his time.

Ashna looked at her watch and it was nearly 1 am. The prawn lady party had just left not before giving a scowl to Jack which brought another smile to Ashna. He thought she was about to erupt in laughter again and then she got a hold of herself.

"Time we left" said Ashna "as we have a 15 minute walk to our rendezvous in Hasni Street." Jack could have sat with her forever. He decided he would make his move tonight so the professional client-adviser relationship would have to take a back seat. Jack paid the bill and left a good tip with a polite thank you for their consideration after they had caused such a mess.

Off they went down the road, heading for what promised to be an interesting end to the evening. Once or twice they thought they heard footsteps behind. Unusual ones as there was an eerie scraping sound with one of the strides as if a heavy boot was being dragged. Every time they stopped to listen it stopped. They decided to dodge down a little side street and then they ran as fast as they could to complete a circle around where they wanted to go. They arrived hot and excited in Hasni Street with 5 minutes to spare and waited under the shadow of an old bus shelter outside the old cinema. 5 minutes went by then 10. They did not speak at all. Suddenly, across the street they saw a match flicker that briefly showed the face of a man in its flame. They both shivered involuntarily and then Jack grabbed Ashna by the forearm and they wandered over.

"Dufforgans" said Jack.

"Of course they are" came the response. They all three relaxed.

The stranger spoke first. "Let's head over there" and he pointed towards the old cinema. They walked quickly and they heard that strange dragging sound again and realised it came from the weird stranger.

"Aha" muttered Jack "so it was you following us awhile back.

"Yep. I needed to be sure no one else was following you. You can be certain they will know where you live and work and probably that you were out for a meal." This made Jack more than a little uncomfortable. The stranger led them through a hole in the wire fence and into the old cinema they went through a door conveniently left open. "I have used this place a lot for drop off points or meetings."

"So what's with the odd code word 'Dufforgans'?" smiled Jack.

"It's an anagram which transposes to 'Snuff Drago'.

"Good Lord. Do you really want to snuff him. Is he that bad?"

"He is worse. I did not carry out one of his requests to 'discipline' one of the other gang members for being late to a meeting and he took a lumphammer to my foot. Was in plaster for 6 weeks and I still cannot walk properly. However, it gives me good status within the gang. Now I'm known as 'Tenderfoot'. Imagine what he would do if he was really mad. OK, now give me the gen."

Jack, feeling slightly queasy, gave him the little information he had on Drago.

"Right," mumbled Tenderfoot, "we need to catch him setting up a deal which means you need to meet him wearing a wire. How do you feel about that?"

"Absolutely great! I cannot think of anything better than trying to record some Slovenian money-laundering, murdering, bloodthirsty psycho drug lord."

"Sarcasm does not become you my friend but it was you who said you needed to remove this guy. Remember?"

The conversation lasted another 20 minutes whilst Tenderfoot persuaded Jack that he would be safe and a dedicated team were behind this operation and would be listening the whole time ready to catch him. He finally agreed even though Ashna wanted nothing to do with it. He just needed the adrenalin rush as he had missed it since he had finished his trick skiing days after a nasty landing halfway up a tree on the side of a mountain. The meeting finally finished after Tenderfoot gave him the wire and lapel mic and told him how to fit it. It was shaped like an old Led Zeppelin rock band's badge. They agreed to liaise through his team leader, Bill (Handsome) Ransom, after the next contact from Drago.

On the way home, Ashna and Jack barely spoke. She was annoyed with him and he was trying to placate her saying at the first sign of trouble he was off. She was not happy and when he took her home she went straight to her front door and went in without even a look back. So much for making a move tonight.

"I feel about as welcome as a porcupine at a nudists' luncheon" was his final thought for the evening.


*Further reading in Appendices Part 1/5*

*More practice Questions and Answers on this chapter in Appendices Part 2.*

## Key Chapter Points

- The basic concept of marginal costing is that we establish the cost of producing or selling one more item.

- The difference between fixed (not reactive to output) and variable (change with output) costs and the fact that no costs are totally one or the other.

- The application of a contribution statement to determining the break-even point or a target profit or sales. B/E = Fixed Costs ÷ Contribution % or Contribution per unit

- The variable costs are assumed to vary in direct proportion to sales. The contribution varies likewise.

- Contribution is useful for making specific decisions on product lines and whether or not to make a product or to supply a product.

- Maximising contribution automatically maximises profit as the fixed costs are sunk.

- Maximising the contribution per scarce resource needs to be considered.

# 13.  Planning and Control through Budgets

Jack did not hear from Ashna for a few days and neither, thankfully, did he hear from Drago. His business was motoring on nicely and he was making money but it all seemed rather haphazard and unplanned. He just seemed to react to every situation that occurred and never really seemed in control. Wally the Waiter was criticising him all the time as he said most of the problems were predictable and Jack seemed to lurch from one financial problem to another.

He decided to call up Ashna and see if she could help. She duly invited him to her office the next day to explain the problems.

He arrived and she looked at him with a mixture of annoyance and sympathy. He knew she was mad at him for getting deeper into this money-laundering issue and he also knew she had feelings for him that he was severely putting to the test.

"It is quite clear that you need some Business Planning help. You need to start by deciding what it is you want to achieve in the long, medium and short term."

"I have only ever worked on what I wanted for the next week. How do I know what I want? I cannot even predict which customers will come into my warehouse from one week to the next."

"Hang on, you have been in business for a year or two now so there must be some kind of trend developing such as good and bad seasons and general growth of the business?"

"Yes, I suppose there is. I know roughly when the good periods are. I also have some idea of where I want to be in 5 years but I have never put it into numbers. I don't know where to begin."

"The bigger the business the further it tends to look ahead. A small business like yours can be quite volatile and reactive to events outside your control. The best way is to decide what your objectives are overall such as making a certain level of profit after 5 years, selling out the company, retiring and leaving the company to family etc. All these long term objectives have different implications for the way you manage the company. For instance, you may want to maximise your personal income for the next two years which will mean drawing out all the profits. This will restrict the company's growth.

A good start is to look at what finance is tied up in the company and then try to achieve a satisfactory return on that total capital as well as a target return on sales. In other words, set yourself a target ROCE ratio (Return on Capital Employed) of perhaps 30% and Return on Sales of at least 10%. So much depends on factors such as the economy, market growth, your own salary etc. and often the simplest is just to go for a good increase on the previous year. This is known as 'Incremental' budgeting where your plan is based upon the previous year and taking into account known changes and then incorporating some performance improvement.

**A budget is often defined as a short term business plan expressed in financial terms.**

The process is as follows:

- Businesses establish their mission and objectives to determine why they are in business and what they want to achieve. This is in the longer term.

- The objectives are then developed into more specific and quantifiable goals.
- Budgets are the **short term** (usually 1 year) means of working towards the business's objectives"

"But is the business going to perform any differently by knowing its budget?" queried Jack.

"Yes it will. For instance, the action of drawing up a budget for the next year will make you think about it. Such as how many products, how many of each, how many staff etc. Your year-end is the end of June so you need to be thinking about your budget for the next year by the end of May. What you then do is break your budget down for the year into the sales, costs of sales, expense headings etc. and break all of these down into monthly figures that you expect to achieve allowing for the profiling of busy and quiet months.  For instance, if 15% of the year's sales were in August this year just gone then you would budget the year's sales for next year and the August budget would be 15% of that figure. This assumes a similar spread of the sales. The variable costs of materials and some of the labour would be similarly profiled as they would react around the sales.

We then need to measure each month what we do in sales and costs, as we do now, but this time compare it with what we thought we would do in the budget. The difference is called a variance.

Here is an example:

|  | Budget | Actual | Variance |
|---|---|---|---|
|  | £ | £ | £ |
| Sales | 21,000 | 25,600 | 4,600 |
| Direct Materials | 1,400 | 1,728 | -328 |
| Direct Labour | 7,000 | 10,200 | -3200 |
| Variable Overhead | 4,200 | 3,840 | 360 |
| Fixed Overhead | 1,100 | 1,150 | -50 |
| Profit | 7,300 | 8,682 | 1,382 |

You can see here that the budgeted sales were £21,000 for the period and we achieved £25,600 so the difference, or variance as it is known, is £4,600. We have gone over budget which for sales has a positive effect on profit so this would be called a favourable variance. If a cost budget went over budget it would be called an 'adverse' variance because it adversely affects the profit. As you can see overall we have a favourable variance from the budget of £1,382 with the sales being very good but the labour budget exceeding the budget by £3,200. Another way of thinking of it is if you take the budgeted profit and add on all the favourable variances and deduct the adverse variances you will get the actual profit."

"Why should the fixed overheads be greater than the budget? Surely they are fixed and so would be on budget?"

"Jack, don't forget that the fixed overheads don't mean that they never change. It just means they do not change with the activity levels. The fixed overheads might be over budget because we have not controlled them properly because we can influence them. For instance, heat and light is a fixed cost but if we turn the lights out earlier at night then we will reduce the cost. It is nothing to do with sales."

"Hold on, hold on" interrupted Jack. "If the sales have increased by over 20% then surely many of the other costs would increase as well. At least that is what you told me before."

"Dead right Jack and this budget is what is called a 'Fixed' budget in that it is fixed or based on an assumed level of activity (in this case sales) and the various departments have a strict level of spending up to which they can go. No more wages and no more materials. It is therefore not a good method if you cannot project the level of activity correctly. We need something more flexible."

"You mean a method that allows the variable costs to move with the activity." Once again Jack had taken Ashna by surprise with his insights.

"You have just about given a definition of a technique called 'flexible budgeting' which was what I was about to explain. The problem with a fixed budget is that if the activity level (e.g. sales) is not predicted accurately then you will be comparing a budget drawn up on sales of, say, £40,000 with an actual situation where the sales are £44,000.

For instance:

Sales & costs for the year are budgeted as follows:

- Sales            £40,000

- Variable Costs    20,000

- Fixed Costs       15,000

Display the variances for sales, costs and profit, If the actuals are as follows:

- Sales            £44,000

- Variable Costs    23,000

- Fixed Costs       15,500

You can see that the actual sales are £4,000 or 10% more than budget. This should mean that the variable costs should be 10% more than the budget so the process we go through is in the following steps:

1. Examine the original budget based on an assumed activity level
2. Compare the activity level of the budget with the actual level
3. Redraw the original budget into a flexed budget as if you 'knew' what the actual activity would be

4. Compare the flexed budget with the actual figures to calculate the variances.

For the example above:

|          | Orig.B  | Flex B  | Actual  | Var      |
|----------|---------|---------|---------|----------|
| Sales    | 40,000  | 44,000  | 44,000  | -        |
| V. Costs | 20,000  | 22,000  | 23,000  | £1,000A  |
| F. Costs | 15,000  | 15,000  | 15,500  | 500A     |
| Profit   | £5,000  | £7,000  | 5,500   | £1,500A  |

So, although the sales have increased, the Variables have increased by a greater proportion & Fixed costs have increased producing an adverse effect on profit!

The original budget now has no purpose except it provides a platform for the calculation of the variable costs. Note that the flexed budget for fixed costs will always be the same as the original budget.

Take a look at this budget statement. The original budget assumed sales of 1400 units whereas 1600 units were sold.

|                  | Original Budget | Flexed Budget | Actual     | Variance |
|------------------|-----------------|---------------|------------|----------|
| Output           | 1400 units      | 1600 units    | 1600 units |          |
|                  | £               | £             | £          | £        |
| Sales            | 21,000          | 24,000        | 25,600     | 1,600    |
| Direct Materials | 1,400           | 1,600         | 1,728      | -128     |
| Direct Labour    | 7,000           | 8,000         | 10,200     | -2200    |
| Variable Overhead| 4,200           | 4,800         | 3,840      | 960      |
| Fixed Overhead   | 1,100           | 1,100         | 1,150      | -50      |
| Profit           | 7,300           | 8,500         | 8,682      | 182      |

Firstly we need to redraw the original budget (column 2) to a flexed budget (column 3) to reflect the 1600 actual units sold. We do this by inflating all the variable figures (including sales) by the effect of the extra 200 units. We effectively add on 1/7th  but the simplest way is just to multiply the original sales budget and variable cost budgets by (Actual activity ÷ Budgeted Activity) = (1600 ÷ 1400). This increases the Sales, Direct materials, Direct Labour and Variable Overheads all in proportion.

We now have a relevant budget which can be compared with Actual figures (column 4) to get a meaningful set of variances (column 5)."

"That all seems to make a bit of sense so is that the whole of budgetary control covered?" Jack was struggling to stifle a yawn.

"There is another method called 'Zero Based' budgeting. This is effectively what happens in a company's first year of operation where it decides what level of service it is going to give and estimates all of its costs based on that. The term is actually used for a similar process applied to an ongoing company situation. You basically start your budgeting from scratch as if you had no previous year's information. It is very time consuming in a large company as you could imagine but has the advantage that it should give a better view of the company's resource requirements and would serve to eliminate any budget 'slack' carried forward from a previous year's 'incremental' budget.

I have put together some notes as usual for you (Appendix Part 1/6) that broadly covers the issues surrounding budgeting such as the benefits and criticisms so I should take a read of it. It should help you in planning and developing with some degree of control. Just remember, you do not always have to stick to the budget if the business environment changes but one thing good business planning does is to make you think deeply about the future and it helps you to recognise changes in the environment as they take place."

Just then, Jack's mobile vibrated and he noticed it was a blocked ID. He answered it and Ashna noticed that he had gone a little pale. He kept nodding and agreeing and finally he clicked the off button.

"What's the matter Jack?" Ashna whispered in a worried tone.

He just said "Drago" and then stared into space. Now she was very concerned. She felt the fine hairs on her forearms stand on end and her breathing came in short shallow sucks.

"What? What's he say? Tell me quickly."

"He says it is time to meet again and the sooner the better if I know what's good for me." All of a sudden Jack leapt out of his seat and knocked all the papers off Ashna's desk and brought his clenched fist down on it so hard that the top splintered and three office staff piled into the room wondering what was going on. He stalked around the room with such a look of aggression and determination on his face that nobody wanted to challenge him. He was letting rip about being fearful in his own country and how he was not going to put up with 'No grizzled, Slovenian headcase who is one French fry short of a Happy Meal is going to tell me what to do." He eventually calmed down and Ashna told the other staff to leave as everything was fine.

"He threatened me" repeated Jack indignantly over and over again. "He threatened me on my own phone. Now I am really mad. He has crept into my life like a furtive animal and he is going to leave it one way or another the same way." Now Ashna realised he was going to do something about it and hoped it was not a rash decision.

"He has asked to meet tomorrow night at 12 midnight at the old cinema in Hasni Street. That is where we met Tenderfoot. What are the chances of him picking the same place? A million to one? I had better contact Bill and quickly."

"Who is Bill?"

"Bill Ransom. Tenderfoot's team leader. You remember, he told us to liaise through him."

## *Further reading in Appendices Part 1/6*

## *More practice Questions and Answers on this chapter in Appendices Part 2.*

## *Key Chapter Points*

- Budgets need to be created with a clear financial goal in mind.

- There is a process in budgetary control that usually commences with a sales budget and finishes with the setting up of the financial plan that is then implemented by the senior managers by reporting through their positions of responsibility.

- Control is exercised through action to improve the significant variances (both favourable and adverse)

- Some budgets are fixed and some are flexible to accommodate changes in the level of activity. (Flexed variable cost calculation: Flexed budget = original budget item X Actual activity ÷ original budget activity)

- There are many benefits and problems with budgetary control and the key to success is involvement and training of the key staff.

# 14. Cash Flow Forecasting

He contacted Bill and they agreed to meet that night. He now understood why Bill was called 'Handsome' Ransom. He was tall, over six feet, athletic, clean shaven, well dressed in some Armani type suit and a very smooth operator. He ran though the procedures with the 'Led Zeppelin' lapel mic, tested it twice and satisfied tried to talk some sense into Jack who had glazed over he was so excited. It felt to Jack as though he was born for this work. He was on a new plane although he was a little concerned at how Ashna appeared to be unable to take her eyes of Handsome Ransom. He realised he was a little jealous. In fact he was jealous to the point of seeing every bit of Bill Ransom as a challenge to his manhood. He questioned everything to the point of annoying Bill intensely. Finally, Ashna told him not to be so stupid and he went a bit sullen but eventually calmed down.

The agreement was that he would meet up with Drago and see how the conversation went. If the team managed to record enough to incriminate him they would all come busting in but otherwise Jack would need to probe a bit to try to get Drago to talk. He was not to forget that Tenderfoot was on the inside. Any sign of physical danger, they would bust in anyway but Jack was to utter the words 'an elephant stood on my hen last week' if he wanted out quickly. He estimated a 30 second wait.

The next day it was tough to settle down to work. Wally was still giving Jack a bit of lip about his planning but Jack assured him it was under way. The day dragged very slowly and he decided to ring Ashna. She was not there and had apparently left the office at lunchtime after a phone call. He tried her mobile which went straight to answerphone. He checked her Facebook page and went cold inside. It just said 'help' on it but it had not been sent to him. Strange. He rang Bill who was quiet at first but said it was probably nothing. And so the moment of reckoning drew near and he still had not heard from Ashna.

He arrived at the old cinema in good time thinking he would do a recce but they were there already perhaps with the same thought in mind. There were two of them with hats pulled down low over their eyes. They came up to him. Both were big and they did not so much introduce themselves as shuffle either side of Jack so that he was effectively manhandled into the old cinema via the same hole in the fence he had used before.

He arrived in a cold, dimly lit area which had a couple of large pillars in the middle and between the two was a man of medium height but with such menace in his face that the blood ran cold in Jack's veins. He had to be Drago and he was proven right as soon as he spoke.

"I am Dragan Kranvogel. We are going to be good partners my hairy friend but I wish to explain my cash flow terms to you first." He beckoned to one of his two stooges. "Vladimar, please fetch the parcel." Vladimar trundled across the floor. He realised that he was not big with fat he was big with muscle but he had obviously fallen out of the ugly tree and hit every branch on the way down. His face was like a bouquet of elbows. He walked behind the pillar and dragged out a chair on wheels and who should be sitting on the chair with a big piece of black tape on her mouth but Ashna. She had a frightened and pleading look in her eyes and Jack could barely face her. He had caused this but they were going to pay …. and pay big time.

"Are you all right?" he asked gently. She moved her head slowly up and down as a tear coursed down her cheek and he turned to Drago. "OK what do you want and just remember that an elephant stood on my hen last week."

"I'm sorry" he said "what did you say?"

"I said that …… "

"It is of no consequence. You will go into a little room until you agree to my cash flow terms. Here is a little reminder of how I negotiate." He tossed a sack containing a heavy, round object. It landed with a heavy thump on the floor. It was the size of a head and Jack went white at the thought of who it belonged to. Also where was the rest of it? He suddenly thought that he had not seen Tenderfoot and feared for his life.

" Vladimar. Take them to the wet cellar."

They were led away wondering what a wet cellar was. They soon found out. It was a cellar that was always wet (this they were told later) and it had a pump in permanent operation to keep the water level down. They passed some very old copper pipes running in all directions and then they sloshed along the wet floor with the filthy, brackish water over their ankles. They came to a halt and Vladimar said appealingly "Sit." Always the one for big words was Vladimar.

They sat on a ledge two inches above the water and Vladimar lashed them to the pipes with a thin piece of rope, removed the tape from Ashna's mouth in an unceremonious fashion and sloshed his way out again. Jack had the feeling he had done this a few times.

"Well, what now? What do you think, Ashna?"

"I think we are in a pickle."

"I think we have them right where we want them. What concerns me is that the back-up guys have not arrived. We need to keep busy. Hey, what did he mean by the cash flow terms anyway?" He had a good idea but he thought it wise to give Ashna something to think about besides her own mortality.

"He probably meant when he put money in to your account, say, £100,000 he would take out £99,000 and leave you £1,000 as a fee for your trouble>"

"Hey, what's so bad about that then?" grinned Jack.

"You mean apart from it being not strictly Beagle?"

"What's a dog got to do with it? Hey, was that your version of Cockney Slang? Beagle, legal ....." They both burst out laughing and didn't stop for quite a few minutes. Thankfully, there was a little light down there and Jack took a long look at her. Even in the state she was in he still thought she was the most beautiful girl, no woman, he had ever seen. He then remembered wishing a while ago that he just wanted to see her looking scruffy for once. Well, he had certainly got his wish and he started to chortle again.

She ignored it and suggested she give him another finance lesson as it looked like they had some time on their hands. So he asked her to tell him a little about cash flow forecasting as Wally the Waiter was beginning to make him feel inferior with all his questions about budgeting and cash planning.

"Right then off we go. Cash Flow Forecasting.

Many people think that because you make a profit you must have more cash in the bank but as we have already learnt when we talked about the Statement of Cash Flows (Chapter 9), a profit does not always mean an improvement in the bank. The first thing to recap is that Statement of Cash Flows (Cash Flow Statements) are historical documents and a part of the annual published accounts that inform you how the Operating Profit translates into the movement in your bank account.

Cash Flow Forecasting is about looking ahead at your monthly bank balance to try to predict what it will be for up to, say, a year. It can be projected weekly, annually or whatever time frame you wish.

Do you remember at University you would receive your student loan in three lumps over the year but your bills were going out every week. This made it hard to balance your money because whilst in theory you may have enough over the whole year after some part-time income and a sub from Mum and Dad, there would be certain times during the year when you virtually run out of money whilst waiting for the second or third 'tranche' of loan.

I just happen to have an example in my jacket pocket but you will have to pull it out with your teeth as I am a bit tied up!"

Jack leaned across and nuzzled his head under her jacket trying to find the paper. It certainly was not the worst experience of his life. That is until she sank her teeth into the top of his skull. "What do you think you are doing Jack it is in my hip pocket!" She exclaimed indignantly.

He felt suitably chastised and managed to retrieve a crumpled bit of paper with figures on it which he dropped onto the floor and smoothed out with his foot.

| RECEIPTS | Sept | Oct | Nov | Dec | Jan | Feb | Mar | Total |
|---|---|---|---|---|---|---|---|---|
| Student Loan | | 1,100 | | | 1,100 | | | 2,200 |
| Part-Time wages | 160 | 160 | 160 | 160 | 160 | 160 | 160 | 1,120 |
| Parent Sub | 100 | 100 | 100 | 100 | 100 | 100 | 100 | 700 |
| Total Receipts | 260 | 1,360 | 260 | 260 | 1,360 | 260 | 260 | 4,020 |
| PAYMENTS | | | | | | | | |
| Food | 300 | 300 | 300 | 300 | 300 | 300 | 300 | 2,100 |
| Books | 280 | | | 280 | | | | 560 |
| Travel Home | 40 | 40 | 40 | 40 | 40 | 40 | 40 | 280 |
| Mobile Phone | 20 | 20 | 20 | 20 | 20 | 20 | 20 | 140 |
| Clothing | 50 | 50 | 50 | 50 | 50 | 50 | 50 | 350 |
| Laundry etc. | 20 | 20 | 20 | 20 | 20 | 20 | 20 | 140 |
| Entertainment | 200 | 200 | 200 | 200 | 200 | 200 | 200 | 1,400 |
| Total Payments | 910 | 630 | 630 | 910 | 630 | 630 | 630 | 4,970 |
| Cash Flow | -650 | 730 | -370 | -650 | 730 | -370 | -370 | -950 |
| Opening Bank | 0 | -650 | 80 | -290 | -940 | -210 | -580 | |
| Closing Bank | -650 | 80 | -290 | -940 | -210 | -580 | -950 | |

Let's just look at this line by line. Remember this is a projection of cash at the bank and not the profit so all the figures should reflect that. Instead of the headings Income and Expenditure as we have in an Income Statement, we call them Receipts and Payments. You can see there are 7 months here September-March and under the Receipts we have the student loan income, the part-time wages and the parent sub. Note the student loan is not averaged over the period but it is what is actually received in the month. There will be one more student loan payment to come in after March. All the Receipts are totalled (down and across).

The Payments are shown mostly going out monthly apart from the books where there are large payments in September and December as you are buying in advance for the two terms. The last figure in payments is the entertainment which is the nights out that I have shown as £50 per week. Clearly this is what might be called discretionary in that it is not essential and you might need to cut back on this part to survive."

"What! Take a cut in the lager department? I don't think so!" Now Jack was becoming agitated.

"In that case you need to up the income so either you earn more wages or tap up Mater and Pater for an extra sub!!

You total up the Payments (down and across) like the Receipts and then deduct each month's payments from the Receipts to arrive at the 'Cash Flow'. For instance, September is £260 Receipts less £910 Payments making a Cash Flow of £650 negative. A bad month. As you can see, October and January are the only positive months as those are when the Student Loans come in. If you total the Cash Flow line across to -£950, this will also give you the total of the Receipts (£4,020) less the total of the Payments (£4,970) so it all balances up.

Having arrived at the Cash Flow for each month we now use this figure to operate on the bank balance. So I have assumed the bank figure starts as zero at the beginning of September (Opening Bank row). The Cash Flow for September is -£650 so the closing balance (Closing Bank row) is -£650. This then becomes the next month's Opening Bank as if the closing bank on September 30th is -£650, this must be the Opening Bank on October 1st. In October there is a positive Cash Flow of £730, so now the bank balance moves to £730 - £650 = £80. Therefore, we add the Cash Flow for a month to the Opening Balance for that month to get the Closing Balance for that month. This then becomes the Opening Balance for the next month and so on. What do you think?"

"I think I drank too much lager at Uni" laughed Jack with a macho expression on his face which Ashna did her best to ignore but she did find it childishly funny all the same.

"Is that all there is to it then? That seems a little simple."

"O.K. What would you do if you only have an overdraft facility at the bank of £500?"

Jack had a look at the closing bank balance for each month. "Well, the bad months are September, December, February and March. I either need to ask the bank for more during those months or spend less until April when my next student loan tranche is received. I could easily delay purchasing the December books to January. I would need to find where the library is for that month I guess. Certainly the 'entertainment' would need to be cut."

"It is a bit of a simple situation so why don't we look at how it is done in a business situation. There is some more in my pocket Jack. Please do the honours again."

His face lit up and then she said "The hip pocket Jack, the hip pocket." He leaned over and managed to retrieve a second piece of paper from her pocket with the aid of his teeth and his chin. He was really warming to this cash flow teaching.

She started "Firstly, we commence with Opening Monetary position – cash balance, accounts receivable (debtors), accounts payable (creditors) then we superimpose Projected Income Statement–adjusted for timing differences making sure that we remove non-monetary items such as depreciation as that is not paid to anyone. We then add in non-Income Statement items such as loan repayments and capital items.

E.G. (one month's credit)

|  | March | April | May | June |
|---|---|---|---|---|
| Sales Invoicing | £1,000 | 1,300 | 1,400 | - |
| Cash Received | - | 1,000 | 1,300 | 1,400 |

So when you sell £1,000 in March it is received in April if it is on a month's credit. If two months credit then it would be received in May. Note that there is no money shown received in March. Why is that Jack?"

"I guess it is because it is a new business as otherwise any sales in February would be received in March."

"Bang on and we would call the February sales money not yet received as Opening Accounts Receivable (Debtors). We would also do the same with the opening Accounts Payable.

Now let's look at the profit forecast.

|  | Jan | Feb | Mar | Total |
|---|---|---|---|---|
| • INCOME |  |  |  |  |
| Sales Revenue | 3000 | 4000 | 5000 | 12000 |
| Other |  |  |  | 0 |
| Total Income | 3000 | 4000 | 5000 | 12000 |
| • EXPENDITURE |  |  |  |  |
| Materials | 1500 | 2000 | 2500 | 6000 |
| Wages | 300 | 300 | 300 | 900 |
| Overheads | 100 | 100 | 100 | 300 |
| Bank Int | 30 | 30 | 40 | 100 |
| Depreciation Fixed Assets | 100 | 100 | 100 | 300 |
| Loan Interest | 30 | 30 | 30 | 90 |
| Total Exp | 2060 | 2560 | 3070 | 7690 |
|  |  |  |  |  |
| Monthly Profit | 940 | 1440 | 1930 | 4310 |

This needs to be turned into a cash flow forecast but we also have other information as follows:

- Opening Accounts Receivable are £4,000 of which $\frac{1}{4}$ is due within one month and the rest within 2 months.
- Opening Accounts payable are £2,000 payable within one month
- Opening Bank balance is £2,000 overdrawn with another £500 cheque to a supplier still not presented.
- There was a purchase of Non-Current Assets for £2,000 paid in February.
- Sales and Material purchases are both on one month's credit
- There was a monthly loan repayment of £170 additional to the £30 loan interest.
- Bank Interest is payable quarterly in arrears (at the end of the quarter).
- There is a tax refund expected in March

It would look as follows:

| | Jan | Feb | Mar | Total |
|---|---|---|---|---|
| • RECEIPTS | | | | |
| Ac Receivable* | 1000 | 3000 | | 4000 |
| Sales Revenue | | 3000 | 4000 | 7000 |
| Other | | | 1000 | 1000 |
| Total Income | 1000 | 6000 | 5000 | 12000 |
| • PAYMENTS | | | | |
| Ac Payable* | 2000 | | | 2000 |
| Materials | | 1500 | 2000 | 3500 |
| Wages | 300 | 300 | 300 | 900 |
| Overheads | 100 | 100 | 100 | 300 |
| Bank Int | | | 100 | 100 |
| Purchase FA | | 2000 | | 2000 |
| Loan Repaid | 200 | 200 | 200 | 600 |
| Total Payments | 2600 | 4100 | 2700 | 9400 |
| Cash Flow | -1600 | 1900 | 2300 | 2600 |
| Opening Bank* | -2500 | -4100 | -2200 | |
| Closing Bank | -4100 | -2200 | 100 | |

Note the items marked with a * are the opening position – receivables, payables and bank balance.

- The bank balance has been adjusted by the unpresented cheque to treat it as it is assumed to have been taken from the bank.
- The materials and the sales have been 'shunted' one month forward to allow for the credit period.
- The bank interest has all been paid at the end of the quarter
- The loan repayments and interest are one payment of £200 (£170 principal + interest of £30)
- The tax refund and purchase of Fixed (non-current) asset are shown in the appropriate months.
- The bank comes into credit of £100 by the end of March.

The big question is whether the bank will lend the maximum borrowing requirement of £4,100 or do we need to find funds from elsewhere?"

"So those gaps we see in January for Materials and Sales Revenue are really filled by the Accounts Payable and Accounts Receivable then?"

"Exactly Jack. The Accounts Receivable and the Sales Revenue could be on one line. They are just separated for ease of demonstration as they are all sales revenue. Similarly, the Materials and the Accounts Payable although the Accounts Payable could contain other bills owing besides materials but the principle is still the same. I will send you some notes on all of this (Appendix Part 1/7) if we manage to get out of this alive." She suddenly started to shiver and her voice went shaky.

From the distance they heard a sound of a door and then a clomp, clomp, clomp, as somebody's footsteps approached. It turned into a slosh, slosh, slosh, as he worked his way towards them through the cellar. It was not Vladimar though. It was the other one. Jack had heard his name in a conversation and it sounded like Sergei but he could not be sure. Jack had always thought it was a nice name until this evening. Sergei stood in front of them looking down. His face looked like he had overdosed on botox because when he spoke nothing in his face moved except his mouth and that seemed under sufferance.

"It is time." Another monotonous voice the owner of which had clearly dropped out of charm school very early on. He bent down and grabbed Ashna roughly around the shoulders and out of his belt he pulled the biggest knife Jack had ever seen. It had a heavy jagged edge and it shone brightly even in that poorly lit cellar. Jack thought he probably looked after it very well and cleaned it every day unlike himself judging by the malodourous hum in the air which seemed to follow him. It was a frightening moment as Jack tried to lean over to somehow protect Ashna and Sergei swatted him away like a fly with a flat slap on his face. Ashna screamed and then down went the knife at speed passing Ashna by a whisker and slashing through the rope securing her wrists to the pipes. His own bonds slackened at the same time and he pulled himself free rubbing his wrists to get the circulation back into them. Sergei was holding each of them by the scruff of their coats and they were dragged out of their potential watery grave. They arrived back in the room with the pillars and there was Drago looking all cool and self-righteous as if he was the nicest person in the world.

"Vell? Hef you thought about my offer? Vill you allow me to use your bank to channel some money for my friends or not?"

Jack needed to keep the conversation going as he did not want to find himself staring out of a sack wondering where the rest of his body was.

"I vill, I'm sorry I will consider it but where is the money going?"

"My friends in Chechnya for a start and also Afghanistan, Turkey, Iraq in fact anyvere zat zey vant to blow somesing ap."

"Ahh. You mean terrorists."

"Maybe. I just like seeing stuff blown up. Perhaps I blow up your house or maybe your dog."

"I don't have a dog."

"O.K. I semtex your goldfish zen. Enough of this."

Whilst Jack was dwelling on how Drago knew about his goldfish or if it was just a lucky guess, the door burst open and Jack realised the cavalry had arrived, led thankfully by Tenderfoot. Whose head was in the sack then? Drago went to his pocket for a gun and Jack threw himself on top of Ashna pinning her to the ground. He thought ruefully that this was something he had wanted to do ever since he met her although in somewhere a little more comfortable. The rest was a bit of a blur. Vladimar went for his gun which was a huge old Colt 45 which got stuck in his waistband and went off with a very loud report and smell of cordite. He managed to shoot himself in the foot putting him temporarily out of action. Sergei bolted through the back of the building and was not found and Tenderfoot gave Drago a little lead ventilation through the arm just to quieten him down. They were safe at last and amid the sirens of police and ambulances they sat quietly holding hands for over an hour. Speech seemed superfluous.

*Further reading in Appendices Part 1/7*

*More practice Questions and Answers on this chapter in Appendices Part 2.*

## Key Chapter Points

- Cash budgets are part of the overall budgetary control process

- They are the financial results of all the other budget decisions.

- The purposes are to ensure the planning and control of the cash resources.

- The opening position is made up of the bank, debtors and creditors.

- The creditor payments are where control on the bank balance is exercised.

- The cash flow is different from the profit forecast because of - timing of receipts and payments, depreciation, capital purchases, loan repayments, refunds and sale of assets.

- The monthly cash flow highlights the good and bad months.

- The bank facility is what we are allowed to borrow not what we are borrowing.

- Long term assets should be financed by long term finance.

# 15. Capex Appraisal Techniques

Life felt a little surreal after that and Jack struggled to come to terms with what had gone on. He regularly called Ashna who said she felt the same and both of them buried themselves in their respective jobs. Jack's business was growing by the week and he had replaced his 'old banger' of a car with a nice new white Audi A5. It looked the business and he could not wait to take Ashna out in it although he had a sneaking feeling that she might think it was a little bit wasteful. Hey ho, that is what accountants are for …. to tell you not to spend anything!

Over a few weeks , he had been chatting with a big brand potential customer, Hedgehog Sports who bought many jumpers from him thanks to a great introduction from Ben Crustybonce, his former employer and they had suggested they would like him to manufacture especially for them. They were offering him a five year contract to supply printed sweatshirts. He was offered the possibility of a great deal of work but he would have to set up a small dedicated production line with specialist overlocking sewing machines and screen printing machines. They would give him a price of £9 per jumper and a guarantee of a minimum of 30,000 units per year to be delivered evenly every month. He had to buy machinery, raw materials and pay extra wages and was very unsure about where to go with the figures.

He was very excited at the prospect but knew it was time to meet Ashna again as he recognised the importance of getting the figures clear before he accepted the contract. He gave her a ring and she was free to see him in her office early afternoon on Friday the next day. She said she was looking forward to it which gave him a huge lift.

The next day he went home at lunchtime having given instructions to Wally, who had now been promoted to his personal assistant, to keep the boat afloat as there were some rush orders to get out as soon as possible. He decided to put on a suit. He did not know why only that he always felt so scruffy when he saw Ashna as she was always so smart and deep down he really wished to impress her and perhaps convey a seriousness about his working relationship with her.

He arrived in her reception area and the receptionist barely recognised him and he waited for her patiently. She was very late coming through and seemed a little upset but he thought nothing of it because she immediately commented on his attire with the words "My, my, you scrub up well, don't you?"

He made no reply other than allowing a wry smile to cross his face. Objective one achieved! He outlined the situation with Hedgehog Sports and she was quiet for a few moments and then adopted her teaching face which she always put on before putting him through his finance paces.

"The first thing is to put together all the Income and Cost figures of the project and create a cash flow forecast for the project. This is actually the hardest part of the whole thing so what figures do you have?"

"I have priced the machinery at 2 screen print machines @ £40,000 each and 4 over-locking sewing machines @ £5,000 each making a total of £100,000. On top of that there are the wages of 6 staff. We need 2 screen printers @ £36,000 each and 4 over-lockers @ £20,000 each. These figures include all their NI costs and also company pension contributions. There is a machinery maintenance contract of 5% of the machinery value which seems sensible and the raw materials will be about 30% of the selling price. There is also the rental of the manufacturing space but I am not sure how to deal with that either."

"Jack, you have done a great job here. We can put all this together easily in a couple of minutes but before we do let's talk about the rental of the floor space. Are you renting further space in which to do the manufacturing?"

He shook his head. "No, we have loads of space in our present premises."

"In that case, for the purpose of making a decision on whether or not to go ahead with this project, we can ignore the proportion of the rent as you will be paying that whether or not you proceed with the project. In other words, the rent is not a 'relevant' cost for the project unless you had an alternative use for it. In assessing projects of this sort we only examine the changes in costs (or income) as a result of the project. We are effectively looking for the 'Contribution' from the project to the company's overall profits." Jack nodded as he could understand that he would not pay more rent by taking on the contract.

"Right we shall summarise the costs.

The total capital costs are 2 print machines @ £40,000 = £80,000 and 4 over-locking machines @ £5,000 = £20,000 so the total capital cost is £100,000. That's a nice round figure and it is this figure which is your benchmark amount that you need to get back so let's look at the operational income and costs.

| | | |
|---|---|---:|
| Income 30,000 units @ £9 per Jumper = | (A) | £270,000 |
| Costs | | |
| Materials @ 30% of sales (30,000 @£2.70) | | 81,000 |
| Wages - 2 printers £72,000 and | | |
| 4 sewing machinists £80,000 | | 152,000 |
| Maintenance | | 5,000 |
| Total Annual Costs | (B) | 238,000 |
| Annual Cash Flow (A-B) | | £32,000 |

There we go. The cash flow is well positive."

It didn't seem a great deal to Jack once all the costs had been removed but at least he knew the worst. "So what do we do with this figure now?"

"We now have the option of using a variety of techniques which we can look at one by one. Payback, Accounting Rate of Return (ARR) and 2 Discounted Cash flow techniques of Net Present value (NPV) and Internal Rate of Return (IRR).

Payback – this means how quickly do you get your money back? So the Capital Outlay is £100,000 and the annual Cash Flow is £32,000.

We can arrange it either vertically or horizontally across the page and note we start with year 0 which basically means today so we commence with the outlay of the capital of £100,000 and then see when we get that sum back by cumulatively adding the annual cash flows:

|        | Cash flow  | Cumulative CF |
|--------|-----------|---------------|
| Year 0 | (100,000) |               |
| Year 1 | 32,000    | (68,000)      |
| Year 2 | 32,000    | (36,000)      |
| Year 3 | 32,000    | (4,000)       |
| Year 4 | 32,000    | 28,000        |
| Year 5 | 32,000    | 60,000        |

So, Jack when do we get the capital back?"

"Well, that is easy. After 3 years we have almost got it back apart from £4,000 so it is early into the fourth year. In fact being a maths genius if we assume that the money comes in evenly throughout the year we could say that the £4,000 as a proportion of year 4 cash flow is 4,000 ÷ 32,000 = 1/8 of a year which is $1\frac{1}{2}$ months. So the Payback is 3 years and $1\frac{1}{2}$ months."

"I never realised you were so pompous but brilliant work anyway. The formula is to take the point where the cumulative cash flow turns from negative to positive. The last negative point was at 3 years and then we add the shortfall (£4,000) as a proportion of the following year's cash flow (£32,000). Bear in mind that the cash flow will often be different in each year as this is a simplistic situation. The other thing to remember is we do not include depreciation of the equipment as a part of our costs. We are dealing with only cash flows and not profit flows here. It is about how quickly our cash outlay is recovered.

This method is used extensively across small and large organisations as it is simple to use and understood by most people not just financially trained ones. It is usually used as a 'first filter' method in that a company will set a maximum payback period of, say, 4 years so that any project that does not pay back within 4 years would not be considered. In your case it pays back in just over 3 years so if the cut off was 4 years you would consider it but if the cut off was 3 years you would not. If you are short of cash you would set the cut off, or 'hurdle rate' as it is known, at a very short time because you want your money back quickly. This is a very simple method to make a quick assessment but it gives no judgment as to the overall profitability of the project but it does address the importance of getting your money back quickly and so considers the riskiness of a project."

"I can use this one. In fact I think I have already used it. Last time I bought a small tool at work for £300, I knew it would save 4 hours work a week for an employee @ £10 per hour so my payback was 7.5 weeks."

"Good example provided the employee's time saved was spent on something useful. Otherwise it saved you nothing."

"No need to be miserable about it."

"OK just making the point. Now we need a method that also considers the whole life of the project. The simplest method is called Accounting Rate of Return or ARR as it is known. Let us look at the cash flows again:

|        | Cash flow |
|--------|-----------|
| Year 0 | (100,000) |
| Year 1 | 32,000    |
| Year 2 | 32,000    |
| Year 3 | 32,000    |
| Year 4 | 32,000    |
| Year 5 | 32,000    |

This method effectively takes the average annual profits after depreciation and expresses this as a percentage of the average capital tied up in the project. So let's look at the average profits first."

"Surely that is £32,000 though.

"Don't forget I said after depreciation. The £32,000 per year excludes depreciation so we need to deduct the yearly depreciation on the machinery. £100,000 over 5 years is £20,000 per annum so that means the average annual profits are £32,000 - £20,000 = £12,000. If you know you are writing off the machinery completely over the project life then the simple calculation is to add up all the cash flows of £32,000 x 5 yrs = £160,000 and deduct the total cost of the machinery £100,000. This gives £60,000 ÷ 5 yrs = £12,000 per annum.

We now need to work out the average capital tied up in the project. The capital at the beginning and end are what, Jack?"

"At the beginning, it must be £100,000 put in for the machinery and at the end it has been completely depreciated so it must be zero."

"Ok. So the average must be (£100,000 + 0) ÷ 2 = £50,000. In other words we just take half of the capital cost when it is fully written off. Now we just express the average profit of £12,000 as a percentage of the average capital of £50,000 which gives:

£12,000 ÷ £50,000 x 100 = 24%

We can now compare this 24% with the cost of our finance. So if we are borrowing money from the bank at 8%, then we are making (24% - 8%) = 16% surplus after financing costs. We do not put in the cost of finance into our cash flows as otherwise we would be accounting for it twice if we then compare with the cost of finance."

"Can you give me a simple one to try out then?" Jack was still eager to prove his abilities to Ashna.

"Right. Try this one.

A project costs £80,000 and the cash flows are:

Year 1    12,000
Year 2    28,000
Year 3    32,000
Year 4    24,000

The company's cost of finance is 12% so should it go ahead?"

Jack got into overdrive. "Well the total of the 4 years' cash flows is £96,000 and we deduct the capital assuming it is all written off. This leaves £16,000 surplus over 4 years which averages £4,000. Divide this by half the cost of £40,000 and we have:

  £4,000 ÷ £40,000 x 100 = 10%.

This is less than the cost of finance so it is not worth doing. Aha. I am the champion of the world." He mimicked a character with a Russian accent from a James Bond film.

"Perhaps. In simple profit terms it is not viable but what if we need to go ahead for a legal or social reason, such as putting in a new staff canteen. Also, if we have a choice of two or more mutually exclusive projects then you would choose the project with the highest percentage return.

We might well also use payback alongside the ARR method. If we have two projects with equal ARR % the project with the shortest payback would be chosen. In the example we have just examined, the payback is well into the fourth year but suppose the cash flows for year 1 and year 4 are reversed. In that case, the payback would be well within 3 years."

"In other words, using payback alongside ARR gives us a better decision. What if one has a better payback and one has a better ARR, how do we make a judgment then?"

"Good question, Jack and that brings us onto the third main method which allows for this. ARR tends to only be used by smaller companies as a quick and easy method and is not particularly helpful on big projects where the capital is not just put into a project at the beginning. This new method using the Discounted Cash Flow technique allows for the time value of money. In other words, £10,000 received today is worth more to us than £10,000 received in a year's time. Any thought why, Jack?"

"I guess because of inflation and you could buy more with the same money today than in a year's time."

"That is true Jack but there is a simpler way of viewing it based on the opportunity cost of getting the money in a year down the way. If you have £10,000 today and your company was in overdraft costing 10% per annum, what would the £10,000 be saving you by getting it in today instead of next year?"

"If you had £10,000 today and it is saving you 10% finance costs for a year, that would be 10% of £10,000 = £1,000"

"In other words, £10,000 today is worth the same to you as £11,000 in a year's time because if you had it today you effectively turn it into £11,000.

If you have £100 today and invest it at 10% it is worth £110 in a year and in two years it is worth not £120 but £121. Why is that Jack?"

"Simple for a maths major. It is compound interest. To add on 10% interest you multiply by (110 ÷ 100). So in the second year we receive interest on the interest. £100 plus 10% is £100 x (110 ÷ 100) = £110 in year one and in year 2 it is £110 x (110 ÷ 100) = £121."

"I sometimes find your level of pomposity staggering beyond belief" laughed Ashna playfully. "Let's turn to how we can use this principle. We are saying that £110 received in one year is worth £100 to us today and that £121 received in two years is worth £100 to us today. To get from today money to one year money we multiply by (110 ÷ 100) = 1.1. Therefore to get from one year money back to today money we do this in reverse. i.e. we divide the money received in one year by 1.1 which is the same as multiplying by (1 ÷ 1.1) = .909. So if we multiply year one money of £110 by 0.909 we get £100 in today money. Similarly for money received in two years. £121 is multiplied by (1 ÷ 1.1) and again by (1 ÷ 1.1) = $(1 \div 1.1)^2$ or 0.826. This means that any money received in one year should be multiplied by 0.909 and in two years by 0.826. These are known as the discount factors so that the further ahead the money is received the more the money is discounted. Also, if the cost of the capital was 20% rather than 10% the factors would change to (1 ÷ 1.2) = 0.833 for year 1 and 0.694 so again would be discounted more. This tells you that the higher the cost of capital, the more beneficial it is to get the money in early. We can take a look at how we would apply this but bear in mind you can always look up the factors in discount tables rather than having to work them out. Here is an example:

| Rate | 2% | 4% | 5% | 6% | 8% | 10% | 12% | 14% | 15% | 16% | 18% | 20% |
|---|---|---|---|---|---|---|---|---|---|---|---|---|
| Year | | | | | | | | | | | | |
| 1 | 0.980 | 0.962 | 0.952 | 0.943 | 0.926 | 0.909 | 0.893 | 0.877 | 0.870 | 0.862 | 0.847 | 0.833 |
| 2 | 0.961 | 0.925 | 0.907 | 0.890 | 0.857 | 0.826 | 0.797 | 0.769 | 0.756 | 0.743 | 0.718 | 0.694 |
| 3 | 0.942 | 0.889 | 0.864 | 0.840 | 0.794 | 0.751 | 0.712 | 0.675 | 0.658 | 0.641 | 0.609 | 0.579 |
| 4 | 0.924 | 0.855 | 0.823 | 0.792 | 0.735 | 0.683 | 0.636 | 0.592 | 0.572 | 0.552 | 0.516 | 0.482 |
| 5 | 0.906 | 0.822 | 0.784 | 0.747 | 0.681 | 0.621 | 0.567 | 0.519 | 0.497 | 0.476 | 0.437 | 0.402 |
| 6 | 0.888 | 0.790 | 0.746 | 0.705 | 0.630 | 0.564 | 0.507 | 0.456 | 0.432 | 0.410 | 0.370 | 0.335 |
| 7 | 0.871 | 0.760 | 0.711 | 0.665 | 0.583 | 0.513 | 0.452 | 0.400 | 0.376 | 0.354 | 0.314 | 0.279 |
| 8 | 0.853 | 0.731 | 0.677 | 0.627 | 0.540 | 0.467 | 0.404 | 0.351 | 0.327 | 0.305 | 0.266 | 0.233 |
| 9 | 0.837 | 0.703 | 0.645 | 0.592 | 0.500 | 0.424 | 0.361 | 0.308 | 0.284 | 0.263 | 0.225 | 0.194 |
| 10 | 0.820 | 0.676 | 0.614 | 0.558 | 0.463 | 0.386 | 0.322 | 0.270 | 0.247 | 0.227 | 0.191 | 0.162 |

Incidentally, the formula for the factor is $1 \div (1+r)^n$ where r is the rate of discount and n is the number of years.

You can see that the factors get smaller with higher rates or higher years.

So if we look at a simple problem to apply, suppose a project lasting 4 years cost £3,000 today and we get £1,000 per year from it and the cost of finance is 10%, is it worth going ahead?

The layout is like this:

| | Cash Flow | | Discount Factor | Present Values |
|---|---|---|---|---|
| Year 1 | £ | 1,000 | 0.909 | 909 |
| Year 2 | £ | 1,000 | 0.826 | 826 |
| Year 3 | £ | 1,000 | 0.751 | 751 |
| Year 4 | £ | 1,000 | 0.683 | 683 |
| | | | Total Present Values | £3,169 |
| | | | Less Capital Cost | £3,000 |
| | | | Net Present Value | £169 |

Firstly, we need a cash flow column followed by a column for the discount factor, which is based on, in this case, 10% finance cost (see highlighted factors in the previous table). These two columns are multiplied out to arrive at the Present Values or Discounted Cash Flows (DCF). From the sum of these (£3,169) we deduct the upfront capital cost to get £169 Net Present Value. So what does this tell us Jack?"

"You don't let me go to sleep do you. Fancy a coffee?" She scowled. "Ok then. The total of the cash flows for the project life are £4,000 and the payback is obviously 3 years. If the total of the present values is £3,169 that means we are making a surplus of £169 which means the project is feasible and is making more than the 10% cost of finance" he said very smugly.

"You can be painful when you are right so often. So if the project cost you £3,169 it would be a zero NPV and effectively the project would be making you exactly the same rate as the cost of the finance i.e. 10%. This is called the Internal Rate of Return (IRR) and not to be confused with ARR. The project actually yields 12.6% IRR which we shall not bother calculating here as in practice you would just use the function =irr(b2:b6) where b2 is the cell with the capital outgoing and the others are the cash flows by year as follows:

| 1 | B |
|---|---|
| 2 | -3,000 |
| 3 | 1,000 |
| 4 | 1,000 |
| 5 | 1,000 |
| 6 | 1,000 |

I have included the formula to manually calculate IRR in the notes (Appendix Part 1/8) but this is never used in practice as the Excel function takes care of it quickly and more accurately.

Why don't you have a go at one Jack?

Here, a company wants to buy a machine costing £5,000 and has cash flows as follows:

| Year | Cash Flows |
|---|---|
| 0 | -5,000 |
| 1 | 2,000 |
| 2 | 1,500 |
| 3 | 1,000 |
| 4 | 1,000 |
| 5 | 1,000 |

Its cost of capital is 14%. Note we have put the capital outlay in as year 0, which means it is undiscounted so is added in (as a negative) rather than deducted at the foot. Work out if the NPV gives a positive decision and also whether it would it be different if it was a cost of capital of 10%. Take the factors from the table above."

Jack sprang to the challenge.

"OK the layout as before would be at 14% finance as follows:

| Year | 14% Cash Flows | Factor | DCF |
|---|---|---|---|
| 0 | -5,000 | 1 | -5,000.00 |
| 1 | 2,000 | 0.877 | 1,754 |
| 2 | 1,500 | 0.769 | 1,154 |
| 3 | 1,000 | 0.675 | 675 |
| 4 | 1,000 | 0.592 | 592 |
| 5 | 1,000 | 0.519 | 519 |
| | | NPV | -305 |
| | | IRR | 11.02% |

But at 10% would be:

| Year | 10% Cash Flows | Factor | DCF |
|---|---|---|---|
| 0 | -5,000 | 1 | -5,000.00 |
| 1 | 2,000 | 0.909 | 1,818.18 |
| 2 | 1,500 | 0.826 | 1,239.67 |
| 3 | 1,000 | 0.751 | 751.31 |
| 4 | 1,000 | 0.683 | 683.01 |
| 5 | 1,000 | 0.621 | 620.92 |
| | | NPV | 113 |
| | | IRR | 11.02% |

Presumably, this means that at 14% finance cost, it is not feasible as it gives a negative NPV of £305 whereas at 10% it gives a positive NPV of £113 and so is feasible. In other words, if you are borrowing money at a higher rate it will have an adverse effect on the likelihood of the project proceeding. How's that, Ashna. Full marks for me, eh?"

"You're insufferable! Unfortunately, you are correct. The IRR of the project is 11.02% and this figure should be compared with the cost of the finance. Clearly, if the project yields 11.02% and the finance cost is 14% then again it is not feasible, whereas at 10% it is feasible. I suggest you have a go at some of the other questions enclosed as well as this also shows how to compare different projects. In principle, you would go for the project with the highest NPV or the highest IRR. Remember, the NPV gives an absolute surplus (or deficiency) in today money terms **after discounting at the cost of capital rate**. The IRR gives a percentage return which can be **compared with the cost of capital rate**.

If we apply it to your earlier situation of setting up a production line for £100,000 and getting £32,000 per year for 5 years with borrowing at 8%, this is the result:

| Cash Flow | | 8% | |
|---|---|---|---|
| - 100,000 | | 1 | - 100,000.00 |
| 32,000 | | 0.926 | 29,629.63 |
| 32,000 | | 0.857 | 27,434.84 |
| 32,000 | | 0.794 | 25,402.63 |
| 32,000 | | 0.735 | 23,520.96 |
| 32,000 | | 0.681 | 21,778.66 |
| | | | |
| | NPV | | 27,766.72 |
| | IRR | | 18% |

The NPV is £27,766 so it is a good surplus. You could use the IRR as a barrier or hurdle as you do with the Payback technique. With this one you might have a minimum payback of 3 years but with IRR you might require a minimum return of, say, 15%. This project is making 18% so would be acceptable."

"So what are the big advantages of the NPV method then?"

"The advantages are fairly straightforward. It allows for the time value of money, it is therefore more accurate but slightly more complex, it covers the whole project life and it gives a clear comparison between projects in absolute terms. However, as a method it is not so easy to communicate to non-financial people."

"It is therefore the best one to use then, once you establish that the payback is within the required time?" asked Jack.

"I would say so and particularly where the capital expenditure runs over a period of time. It will make allowance for that as well as the income being received over a period of time."

"I guess we are nearly done today then. How about coming out for a meal tonight as it's Friday and we need to relax. We have not really talked since our encounter with Drago, have we? You also seemed very upset when I arrived. May I enquire as to why?" he said softly.

"I have been 'let go' I think the expression is."

"What, fired!" he exclaimed loud enough to be heard two offices away. "Just let me get hold of whoever did that" Jack was seething with rage.

"Don't bother" she said. I have agreed to go quietly. "I had been pressured to put in false time figures to a major client's audit contract and I refused so someone else in the practice has done it. I have agreed to leave and they have given me a payoff and a reference provided I do not speak to the client. I am very upset as I had faith that my employer had better standards than this. I thought of going to the Association but it is my word against theirs and I probably would not get work in this profession again, at least not in this town. So, Jack I am very upset and really not up for going out for a meal tonight."

"Swine. Who do they think they are?" Jack was frustrated and deeply saddened for Ashna as he knew she was great at her job and how could she now be his accountant? He wandered out of her office after giving her a sympathetic handshake and was buried in his own thoughts as he wandered home. His chest ached and he did not know why.

### *Further reading in Appendices Part 1/8*

## More practice Questions and Answers on this chapter in Appendices Part 2.

## Key Chapter Points

- We need to assess a project for both feasibility and the best out of a 'choice'.

- There are techniques used in the process – Payback, ARR and DCF

- Payback is usually used as a hurdle rate alongside other methods.

- Two methods utilise the time value of money – NPV & IRR

- NPV projects can be assessed on the highest NPV and IRR on the highest percentage

- The IRR occurs when the NPV is Zero.

- The discount rate is based on the cost of capital and determines the discount factor that is used and so allows for the time value of money..

# 16.  Epilogue

Having got home he lay on his bed with his eyes shut. He screwed them up so tight they were watering in the vain hope he would start to feel better. He thought back over the last couple of years to the people he had met.

There was Ben Crustybonce who was his old employer. He had not enjoyed working for him but had learnt a great deal from him. In the end Ben had come good and managed to help him hugely in finding some good customers as Ben's pottery mugs were promotional items in a similar way to some of Jack's. Jack was seriously grateful to Ben and had managed to repay him by passing on some of his clients to Ben when they were in the promotional field and needed mugs with logos in their product range. Ben's latest introduction could make him a great deal of money.

He remembered his old girlfriend, Ziggy Pretzel. He could not imagine what he saw in her and for that matter what she saw in him. He had thankfully had little contact with her but heard that she was now a groupie following some retro punk band called Night Vision Zip Slasher. Good luck to her – it sounded like she needed it.

He thought about his first supplier, Crosby Blob, the local wholesaler. He did not think about him long as he was a wazzack.

He opened one eye briefly and watched Shuggie the goldfish who was still swimming around his bowl in the same direction. He wondered whether he would have anxiety attacks if he went round the other way.

Wally the Waiter was going great guns and after his promotion to personal assistant seemed to have discovered an energy elixir. He was running around the business like a man possessed and had a real eye for fashion. He hoped Wally would stay with him. He would pay for him to do a business training course.

Tenderfoot, the undercover policeman, he assumed was still limping around in the half light. He had a strange liking for this rather shabby individual.

Drago was prosecuted and found guilty of three counts of murder, and also gun-running, drug-dealing, money-laundering, other hyphenated crimes and kidnapping someone's head without their permission.

Merc man thankfully did not run into him again but he did see his name in the papers as having lost his council official's job in the planning department as he had been on the end of an anti-corruption purge.

Vladimar was jailed for being in charge of an unlicensed loaded gun which had more bullets in the magazine than he had points in his IQ.

Sergei was never heard from again but Jack guessed he was doing a Foundation course in moving his face. He doubted he would pass.

Bill (Handsome) Ransom had smoothed his way to the top. He had married the daughter of local landed gentry and then hit bottom as he was caught 'In Flagranti Delicto' with the local Police Commissioner's wife in the back of his 'S' type Jaguar.

That only left Ashna. He could not help thinking about her. Her infectious smile, her straight black hair glistening and shiny, her ready laugh and her beautiful figure. He would miss her. What was he talking about? He leapt off the bad, tripped on an old shoe and drove his head straight through a wooden panel of the wardrobe. That knocked a modicum of sense into him. He knew at that moment of acute pain that he was wildly in love with her. He immediately tried her on the phone without luck so he Facebooked her to plead with her to come out for one last meal as he said he had a big financial problem on which her help was urgently needed. It was blackmail he knew as her professionalism would not allow her to let him down no matter how depressed she felt. It was also a little economic with the truth but 'All's fair in love and war' or so he had heard.

She got back to him within a half hour and they agreed to try yet another restaurant. This time they fixed on a fun place called Chicarito's with a Mexican cuisine and named after a small 'Pisum Sativum'. Also the nickname of a fine Mexican footballer!

He picked her up from her home and he went round to the passenger door to open it for her. He needed to muster every bit of skill, ingenuity and good manners tonight. She looked amazing, dressed in a black trouser suit as if she was in mourning for her job. She still looked a little down in the mouth but managed an admiring look at his new Audi. He could see her adding up the annual depreciation figures though.

"So what is this financing issue Jack? It feels like we are sitting in it."

"Naughty, naughty. Nothing to do with the car. Much bigger than that and I think we need a full stomach for it though, so can we wait until dindins?"

They arrived and ordered drinks and food in some very comfy armchairs whilst waiting for a table. The atmosphere in the restaurant was great but it was not reflected in Ashna's mood. She was quiet, pensive and a little withdrawn. "A Margarita should fix this" thought Jack. The Margaritas arrived with a few dips and thankfully they were gold standard.

"What is in these drinks Jack?"

"Not much, just a little quality Tequila, Grand Marnier, orange juice and lime juice and salt. " He said knowledgably whilst reading the recipe from his Android under the table.

She finished it startlingly quickly and they ordered another one each just as they were called to the table.

At the table, the drinks arrived again and within 5 minutes their main course arrived. It was a sizzling platter of steak strip fajitas in a sauce to die for alongside cheese, lettuce, salsa, guacamole (he loved that word), sour cream and warmed tortillas. The table was cluttered so they downed their drinks quickly again. Ashna started to feel hugely better and they tucked in.

"Now, Ashna, I have a suggestion to make and I hope you will take me up on it because this financing deal was just a ruse to get you to come out with me."

Ashna did not really take it in as her head was spinning in a pleasant sort of way and there was a slight burning sensation from the spices in her mouth.

"I would like you to come and work with me as my full time Financial Director. I know it is not in the profession but we are growing fast and the financial control is everything at this stage in our business aside from which I think I have fallen in love with you." He blurted it all out without a breath.

At this point, Ashna had her mouth full of tortilla, steak fajitas, and lots of sour cream and guacamole. When this mouthful is combined with two quickly drunk Margaritas, being sacked and then a job offer in the same day, no force of nature could have prevented what was going to happen next. She gave one huge cough and out came the lot and it streaked like a missile past Jack's startled face and landed square in the water jug of the next table with a resounding 'plop'. Some of the spray from Ashna's mouthful had caught Jack in the eyes and he was temporarily blinded due to the spicy seasoning. He was in momentary agony and got up quickly with streaming sightless eyes and from there things just got worse. He had unbeknown to him tucked the edge of the tablecloth along with his napkin into the front of his trousers. He spun around seeking help for his painful eyes dragging the total contents of the table onto the floor. As Ashna attempted to prevent the wholesale destruction of yet another restaurant, she reached across the table to quickly to grab the retreating tablecloth and fell onto the table collapsing it and pulling Jack on top of her. The whole restaurant went quiet and even the background music of trumpets playing 'La Cucaracha' provided little help in covering their embarrassment.

The hot platters had mercifully skidded across the floor leaving a ghastly slug-like trail but Ashna in her black trouser suit was splattered in white sour cream, a scenario of which he had often fantasised, and she uttered the fateful words "You sure know how to give a girl a good time."

He looked down at her, placed his hands on either side of her face and kissed her tenderly on the lips. She responded as her whole body melted into his and Jack sensed rather than heard loud applause from the other restaurant guests, at least those not covered in Fajita sauce.

"I'll take that as a yes then" he whispered.

# 17. Appendices Part 1 – Notes

### Appendix 1

Book-keeping systems

"We shall start with the sales side. This part is critical as you need to ensure that you send a bill for everything you despatch from your warehouse and get paid for it. Firstly, a customer will place an order with you, perhaps on the telephone. Ideally, you need a customer order number and a written copy from them that you record when you send them a bill. If they do not use one then note the name of the person giving the order and confirm the details back to them. i.e. the price, the quantity, description and delivery date. When you are a larger company you will produce a Goods Despatch Note (a GDN). This is produced by the warehouse and should match with the customer's order details. The delivery driver should have this signed by the customer's warehouse manager acknowledging delivery. A GDN copy is also sent to the accounts office from which they produce an invoice to send to the customer. An invoice should be on your headed paper with details of the product or service you have delivered, date, volume, price and VAT (sales tax) added so the total is what they should pay you. Also, the settlement terms should be stated and should be agreed beforehand such as payment in 30 days or 2% discount if paid in 7 days. If a customer is unhappy with a product such as if you send them 50 sweaters @ £10 each and two of them are faulty. You have already sent them an invoice for £500 so you need to send them a credit note for the faulty goods. This would be 2 sweaters @ £10 or £20. That is if you cannot send replacement sweaters. So your sales credit notes are deducted from your sales invoices to arrive at your net sales for the period."

"So" thought Jack "an invoice is a demand for payment then?"

"Well not exactly, Jack. An invoice is the basis for payment but often you will send several deliveries to a customer in a month and they may have already paid you for some of them so all these transactions should be summarised in a 'Statement'. This shows all the invoices and payments received and the amount due (because not all the invoices in a month may be due by the month end). It is good practice to send a statement because it acts as a reminder to pay and also it will confirm that your book-keeping is in line with your customers and if not it will help to highlight any errors. Attached to the statement will often be a tear off strip which acts as a 'remittance advice'. This would be enclosed by your customer with their cheque. Increasingly these days, payments are made directly through the bank which means you need a very good referencing system so that you can trace any money received into your bank directly to the customer.

There will be a similar system for purchases. In a larger business when someone wants to buy something for the business they usually have to ask for a purchase order to be raised. There may be a formal form to be completed called a purchase requisition and this will have to be signed by an authorised person. On receipt of a purchase request or requisition the purchasing department will normally raise a purchase order

This document will be addressed to the supplier with details of the goods ordered and the price to be paid. It may also specify payment terms. These details will be on the purchase requisition

The order will have a unique reference number. When the goods are received the receiver normally raises a goods received note (GRN) detailing the items received and the quantity therein and sends it to the accounts department. When the supplier sends an invoice the accounts department check the quantity against the GRN and the price against the order. If it is in order they will normally pay it as it falls due.

If it isn't, they will normally send it to whoever authorised the raising of the order to authorise payment of the revised quantity/new price. Once authorised, it will be paid as and when it falls due. If an invoice is wrong then the accounts department would inform the supplier and ask for a credit note and/or a new invoice.

A Purchase Authorisation form will often be attached to the invoice or may be stamped on it as follows:

- PO Number_____

- Cost Code _____

- Quantity _____

- Price _____

- Authorised _____

Goods can be bought for cash or on credit. If bought on credit the terms should be agreed beforehand. Common terms are 'Payment 7 days from the date of the invoice' or 'Payment 60 days from date of delivery'. They can be much longer and there may discounts offered for early payment such as 3% if paid before the month end. Suppliers often send statements to remind their customers that payments are due (or overdue!). Statements should not be confused with invoices.

## Appendix 2 – Long Term Capital Sources

### Ordinary Shares

Ordinary Shareholders control the company through their voting rights – one vote per share. A company has 'Authorised' Share Capital (in its Memorandum of Association) which is the maximum limit of the shares it can issue. So its Authorised Shares might be 50,000 x £1 shares but it may have issued only 20,000 shares. Therefore if you own 10,001 shares you have over half of the issued shares and voting rights and therefore have day to day control. If you own 75% of the Issued shares (15,000 shares) then you have almost total control as you can change most of the fundamental aspects of the company without the agreement of the remaining shareholders. For instance, you may liquidate the company against their will. The dividend can vary every year so it could be very high or nothing at all making Ordinary Shares potentially risky.

### Preference Shares

Preference shares are issued as for example 8% £1 Preference Shares. This means a fixed 8 pence for every £1 shares held will be paid as dividend each year. They are called Preference Share because their fixed dividend is paid in full before the Ordinary shareholders receive any dividend. Also, they are paid in full on liquidation before the Ordinary shareholders receive any dividend. They do not normally have voting rights like Ordinary shareholders so do not 'control' the company. As they do not normally share in the profits, their return will be less than Ordinary shareholders. They are therefore less risky, have less control and have less return than Ordinary shareholders.

Preference shareholders are actually designer shares and they can have many aspects designed into their construction.

They can be:

- Part-participating or non-participating. Part-participating could be something like if profits are above a certain level then the dividend would also be an extra percentage of the additional profit.
- Cumulative or non-cumulative. Cumulative Preference shares would have any shortfall in a dividend in one year (eg if it was a very bad year) rolled up into the following year's dividend. Non-cumulative would mean if there was no dividend declared one year it would not be added to the next year's dividend.
- Redeemable or irredeemable. There might be a fixed future date when the shares would be purchased back (redeemed) by the company. They could also be redeemed at a premium meaning that they might be bought for £1 each but when redeemed the company would pay, say, £1.30 per share to the shareholder.
- Shares with some attached voting rights. For instance, for every 10 Preference shares held, this might be equivalent to the voting rights of one Ordinary shareholder.
- Convertible Preference shares. The shares might contain an option to convert them into Ordinary shares upon a certain event. For instance, after 10 years or the company hits a certain level of profits or if the company is sold or becomes a Public Company and goes for a stockmarket flotation. The benefit would be a large capital growth for the shareholder with less risk along the way. It is a popular addition to the share with venture capitalists (private equity and loan finance firms).

## Debenture Loan Stock

Loans are not necessarily just loans from a bank. They might be what are known as 'loan notes'. A company might decide not to go to a bank to get a loan but prefer to issue loan notes (or loan stock). They would become holders of loan notes or 'bondholders'. A company could raise, say, £50 million by going to a bank and borrowing at perhaps 10% costing £5 million per year in interest. Instead, it might go to the stockmarket and float 500,000 loan notes of £100 each (they are sold in denominations of £100) at 8%. This would raise (hopefully) all the £50 million required and the interest paid would be only £4 million per annum. This would be attractive to the company as it would pay lower interest and also to the bondholder who would be getting a better rate of interest (perhaps with more risk) than it would get if investing directly in a bank. These loans would still usually be secured on some of the assets of the company.

## Appendix 3 – Medium Term Finance

### Hire Purchase

With Hire Purchase agreements (sometimes called closed end leasing), the hirer (the one using the asset) will own the asset legally after the last payment is made. Until that time, title (ownership) remains with the seller. Normally a deposit is paid and the hirer then pays the balance owing in equal monthly instalments including interest on the outstanding balance. The hirer will have the right to 'pay off' the balance early saving any interest less any reasonable charge for early termination. Despite not owning the asset during the process, the asset will be shown in the Balance Sheet as well as the outstanding balance due to the owner as a liability. It will be depreciated in the normal way and the interest paid will be a charge in the Income Statement.

### Operating and Finance Leases

An operating lease is one where the asset is going to be used for a period that is significantly less than the life of the asset. For example, a business might rent a building for five or ten years. The landlord retains ownership and the tenant (business) pays a monthly or quarterly rent which is a normal expense in the Income Statement. The building would be returned to the landlord at the end of the lease period or a lease extension agreed. It would never show as an asset in the Balance Sheet.

A Finance Lease is where a business (the lessee) leases (rents) an asset for the large majority of its useful life. The ownership remains with the lessor (the finance company) throughout the life of the lease. At the end of the lease, the lessor may sell the item to the lessee but not necessarily. The asset is shown as an asset in the Balance Sheet as well as the outstanding payments with interest showing as a liability (similar to Hire Purchase). Similar to H.P., finance lease expenses are split between interest expenses (on the Income Statement) and repayment of the principal value (on the Balance Sheet). The full finance lease payments are tax deductible and leases in general are undertaken to release cash flow for other aspects of the business.

## Appendix 4 - Short Term Finance

### Short Term Loans

Companies often show short term loans but the reason for this is usually not that a company has borrowed in the short term, remember this means repaying within a year. It is that when we borrow a sum over many years, the part that is repayable within a year is shown as a short term loan. For example, if we borrow £40,000 repayable equally over 5 years this would not show in the Balance Sheet as Non-Current Liability £40,000. It would show as Non-Current Liability £32,000 and Current Liability £8,000 because the £8,000 would all be repayable within one year.

## Bank Overdrafts

If one has a bank 'facility' of £80,000 this means that you can borrow up to £80,000 without getting permission from the bank. The beauty of an overdraft is that you only pay interest on the balance as you use it unlike a loan where you pay interest on the full loan that is outstanding. Also, a bank overdraft is repayable 'at call' meaning the bank can ask for it to be repaid immediately if they so wish whereas a loan is for a fixed period of time.

## Accounts Receivable and Payable - Settlement Discounts

Settlement discounts can encourage customers to pay quickly but if they are fixed too high they can be too costly. For instance, if you offer 2% settlement discount to pay 2 months early to a customer, this equates to 1% per month or 12% per annum. Whilst bank interest rates are low at say 7% then this will be an incentive for them to pay early without it costing you too much (12% - 7% = 5%) but if you offer 2% to pay one month early this equates to 24% so would be costing you a huge 17% effective interest. The same applies to accounts payable. It is always worth paying early provided the settlement discount when annualised (i.e. monthly settlement saving x 12) is greater than the annual cost of bank interest.

## Debt Factoring

Debt Factoring which means the transfer of the accounts receivable to a factoring company is a worthwhile exercise for a company with high margins and a growing turnover. Details from the 'Asset Based Finance Association' website on http://www.abfa.org.uk/public/public.asp

## Appendix 5 - Break-Even Chart

*Break-Even Chart*

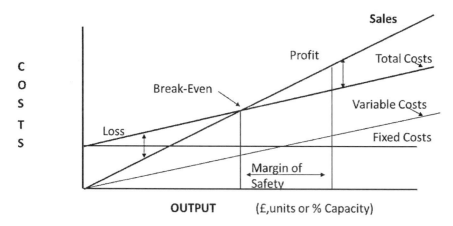

1. The break-even chart serves to demonstrate cost behaviour and therefore shows at what level of output a company attains profitability.

2. The variable costs line angle reflects the proportion of variable costs to sales. Therefore a steep angle indicates a high proportion of variable costs and a flat angle indicates a low proportion.

3. The total costs line is the sum of the variable costs and the fixed costs and is in parallel with the variable costs line.

4. As the sales price increases, the sales line becomes steeper and so the profit at a given level of output increases also lowering the break-even point.

5. The break-even point is the point where the sales equals the total costs.

6. The margin of safety is the difference between the break-even turnover and the current level of turnover.

7. The output can be expressed in number of units, sales value or % of capacity.

8.  It assumes that there is no limit to the relevant range (the range within which the cost structures stay the same) whereas in practice the range is possibly only relevant between + & - 10% of the break-even point.

9. All break-even charts have a similar appearance. They are easily drawn by inserting the fixed costs line and the break-even point. Then draw two more lines through the break-even point with one starting at zero and the other starting where the fixed costs line meets the 'Y' axis.

## Appendix 6 – Budgetary Planning & Control

## What Is Budgetary Control?

Budgetary control is a term used to describe the process of drawing up a plan of how the company is expected to perform in the coming period, usually a year, and then the use of that plan as a measure against which actual performance is judged and the appropriate controlling action taken. There are two key words here and they are 'plan' and 'control'. We draw up a *plan* and then *control* the outcome to ensure that plan succeeds.

## Issues to Consider

There are some key issues involved when we are considering the setting up of a budgetary control system.

## The need for a goal

Like any journey by sea to find the buried treasure on an island, it is important to first know what you are trying to achieve. In other words we set a course to steer from our current position. At the beginning of the process, a business plan is produced which covers the whole of the long and short term objectives and strategy for attaining them. Setting a budget is purely the financial plan incorporating all of those strategies and actions.

The plan is directed to achieving the goal and we need to consider how we are going to achieve the desired outcome such as what resources are going to be needed like finance, machinery or buildings or staff?

We need to consider how we are going to implement the budgetary control process from the point of view of the managers and staff who are affected and whether they will resist the implications.

There is an element of profit planning in the budget. Is it acceptable to the relevant parties such as shareholders, stock market analysts, bankers etc.?

An improvement on the previous year is always desired and this may be shown by utilising ratios primarily driven by Return on Capital and Earnings per Share.

Break-even analysis may also be used to target profit, sales etc.

**Finally we need to Control the Outcome**

There is a need to not only monitor what is done but also to control what is done as the operation proceeds.

This is achieved by means of variance analysis whereby the actual results are compared with the budget to produce a variance report. This is a list of differences or variances from the budget for example here is a report from the sales director for month three in the year:

| Current Month - 3 | | | | Cumulative for three months | | |
|---|---|---|---|---|---|---|
| | Budget | Actual | Variance | Budget | Actual | Variance |
| Promotion | 1,000 | 1,100 | (100) | 3,000 | 2,800 | 200 |
| Advertising | 700 | 500 | 200 | 4,000 | 4,700 | (700) |
| Commission | 2,000 | 4,000 | (2,000) | 6,000 | 10,000 | (4,000) |
| Wages | 5,000 | 5,500 | (500) | 15,000 | 16,500 | (1,500) |
| Totals | 8,700 | 11,100 | (2,400) | 28,000 | 34,000 | (6,000) |

In the current month 3 there is an overspend or 'adverse' variance on all but the advertising but to properly interpret these figures, the year to date needs to be examined as one month on its own may not be truly representative of a trend. In the year to date we can see that the promotion expenses are actually within budget as it shows a positive or 'favourable' variance overall and the advertising is £700 over budget when it was under during the month. These reports are known as variance reports or exception reports in that they sometimes highlight exceptional items automatically by a computer generated variance, which is outside a set tolerance level. Variances may be adverse (if profit is decreased) or favourable (if profit increased). A bracket would denote an adverse variance. In a sales budget, if the budget were exceeded then it would be a favourable variance, which is of course the opposite of an expense budget.

These budget reports would be produced by the management accountant each month and given to the person *responsible* for that section or function. For instance, the sales director receives the sales analysis; the HR director receives the personnel analysis and so on. This is what is known as 'responsibility reporting' where the person responsible reports back on their area of responsibility.

Only the significant variances should be examined (known as management by exception) so as not to waste time examining figures that are close to budget. *All* significant variances need to be explained and this includes the favourable ones as some favourable variances may cause a detrimental effect later. For instance, a favourable advertising variance may show up with a significant reduction in sales the following month!!

At the monthly board meeting, the directors would each report back on their own sections giving reasons for over or under achievement of the budget. If each individual part of the budget is managed successfully then the whole plan should be achieved.

There are many limiting factors which affect the preparation of a budget such as capacity and size of market but an example of the way a budget 'cascades' down from the top is as follows (this assumes sales are the only limiting factor and that, normally speaking, sales are the starting point in a budget because they determine many other factors):

Example for a consumer products company:

## 1. Sales budget

These are broken down by product group and geographic area. Decisions are taken on new products and whether to drop old products.

## 2. Advertising budget

To achieve the sales above an advertising strategy is planned and budgeted.

## 3. Finished Stock Levels budget

To execute the sales we need set stocks available at the end of each month before delivery.

## 4. Production Budget

To achieve the stock levels we need to work out the required monthly production.

## 5. Materials, Labour, plant capacity and overheads

These elements of production all need their own budgets once production requirements are set.

## 6. Cash Budget

This financially ties in all the other budgets together to show the total cash requirements for the period ahead.

## 7. Summary Budget

This breaks down the budget across time periods, divisions, subsidiaries etc.

## 8. Master Budget

This is the one finally adopted when the senior management have adjusted the budget according to what they need to satisfy the investors and other interested parties in the company.

## 9. Responsibility reporting

The budget is then distributed to the relevant senior staff whose job it is to control that budget.

The outcome is then controlled and there are two aspects to this. One is to pinpoint the area of non-performance utilising variance analysis and the other is to take the corrective action.

The interpretation of the variances has already been briefly discussed but success or failure of the interpretation depends on a number of factors, namely:

1. The budgeted figures need to be based on ***accurate standards***. It is no use trying to achieve a budget that is unattainable or based on incorrect figures.

2. ***Forecast variances*** need to be separated from ***performance variances***. By this is meant that in certain cases there will be errors in the budget due to inaccurate predictions such as currency exchange rates. This is a forecasting variance as opposed to perhaps the purchasing of excess material that is a management performance variance.

3. ***Controllable and non-controllable*** costs need to be separated. Managers should not be judged on the part of their budgets over which they have no control (or influence). For instance a manager cannot control the rates paid on a property but the telephone bills can be controlled.

4. ***Some costs will automatically move in line with activity*** (like purchases) and so a fixed budget is not an appropriate control.

## Flexible Budgeting

We have so far been discussing budgets being drawn up which are 'fixed' meaning immoveable. Therefore if a manager does not achieve the budget it is deemed to be poor performance. Clearly, a fixed budget is not always appropriate as some costs move in line with activity. Therefore a refinement of the budget setting we have already examined is to budget a price and a number of units that will then be determined in the budget by the number of units actually achieved.

For instance, you might be running a restaurant and your budget for food in the month is £2,000 based on £2 per customer consuming 1000 meals. Suppose you spend £2,300 but you have served 1,200 customers what should the variance be. If it was a fixed budget you have an adverse variance of £300 (budget £2,000 - actual spend £2,300).

A flexible budgeting approach would review the budget on the basis of number of customers upto 1,200 customers @ £2 = £2,400 and so the ensuing variance would be £100 favourable (budget £2,400 - actual £2,300). For some costs, principally direct costs, this approach is sensible.

Costs can be both fixed, variable and semi-variable where there is an element of both such a phone bill which might contain a fixed line rental and a variable charge for the number of calls. Other semi-variable costs might be electricity bills (lighting is fixed and power is variable), salespersons' wages where they are paid a basic wage (fixed) and a commission (variable) on sales, total wages (fixed but overtime element variable). In this case the cost needs to be 'decomposed' or split into its variable cost per unit of activity and its fixed cost element. The technique can be applied as follows:

Electricity Costs are £5,000 for 2,000 units produced and £7,000 for 3,000 units produced, calculate the variable cost/unit and thus separate out the fixed costs.

Step 1 Increase in costs is £2,000 (£7,000 - £5,000), increase in activity is 1,000 units (3,000 – 2,000)

Step 2 This increase in costs must all be variable so calculate the variable cost/unit by dividing the increase in costs by the increase in units

i.e £2,000 ÷ 1,000 = £2/unit.

Step 3 Apply this variable cost rate to either activity level to work out the variable costs at that level. E.g 2,000 units @ £2/unit = £4,000

Step 4 Deduct the £4,000 from the total costs at that activity level to arrive at the fixed costs. E.g. £5,000 - £4,000 = £1,000 fixed costs. (You can check this at the higher level activity. 3,000 units @ £2 per unit is £6,000 plus £1,000 fixed costs = £7,000 total costs)

## Incremental or zero based budgets

Generally speaking, budgets are drawn up based upon the actual figures achieved in the previous year taking into account any expected changes such as inflation for the following year. This is known as an **'incremental' budget** in that it changes in 'increments' or small movements from the previous year. A problem with this approach is that it will carry forward any weaknesses in the previous year's figures. For instance, if too much has been allowed in the previous year for training costs, the budget may all be spent even if it was not needed. This is where the use of **'zero based' budgeting** (ZBB) may be useful. In simple terms, ZBB means that rather than basing the budget on last year's figures a completely new budget is drawn up with each figure being separately justified in minute detail. This is, of course, what would be done in a company's first year of trading when it has no previous year on which to base estimates. By utilising ZBB it tends to eliminate these carry forward problems but it is very expensive and time consuming to implement and companies tend to use it every few years or so. Alternatively, some companies use it on a different department every year on a rolling basis.

## Benefits And Criticisms of a well organised Budgetary Control system

**Benefits** of a well-run budgetary control system:

1. *Motivation of Staff*

Staff members are motivated to 'beating' the budget assuming that it is realistically set.

## 2. Coordination

All members of staff are pulling together with one agreed goal.

## 3. Communication. The process aids communication between departments who might otherwise not pass information on.

## 4. Delegation

*The* process aids delegation of some duties. For instance, the Human Resource manager can delegate the training budget to the training manager.

## 5. Prioritisation & Resource Allocation

The plan will contain clear priority for certain tasks and resources.

## 6. Decision Making

Many decisions are already made in the budget thus making some decision making easy.

## Criticisms

There are equally some **negative** aspects to budgetary control, particularly if it is not managed well. These are:

## 1. Cost

It can be very expensive in time particularly when standard costing is also included.

## 2. Inflexible & Limit Initiative

It can encourage a hard line approach which can also lead to an 'unthinking' manager who only does what the budget says.

### 3. Defence Mechanism

It can be used as a defence for a bad decision. Many budgets are set up a significant time before the year starts and so the business environment can change and a manager needs to see that **when appropriate** the budget is not adhered to or seek authorisation for alteration.

### 4. Create a Need to Spend

If it is not spent this year it will be reduced for next year. A very common situation with local authority spending and also training budgets.

### 5. Recriminations

Is it fair to use non-performance against a budget as a recriminatory tool? It should be used for improving performance not castigating staff.

### 6. Performance Assessment

Is it fair to judge a manager's performance against a budget that was drawn up 18 months ago when the business environment may have been different?

*The key to successful implementation of a budgetary control system and to avoid the above problems is to train the staff involved in the process and to ensure that those charged with the task of managing a budget are involved in the process of designing and preferably agreeing the budget in the first place.*

## Appendix 7 - Cash Flow Forecasting

What is a Cash Budget?

A cash budget is a projection (usually monthly, quarterly, annually) of the company's cash position based upon _expected_ income and expenditure over the period.

It is easiest to think of budgeting in your private capacity and then to turn it into a business situation.

You have, say, £1,000 in the bank on the first of the month but you need to allow for a cheque for £100 which you have issued for a meal at Macdonalds which has not cleared your bank. This means you realistically have £900 to spend. Your salary cheque for £2,000 is due in on the 3rd of the month giving you an expected total of £2,900 but you also have standing orders and direct debits of £1,200 for your mortgage, £500 for your life assurance and another £500 for electricity, rates and sundries. You therefore have an estimated available spending power of £700 in the month. The question is can it all be used on having fun? The answer is clearly no because the other bills which you will have to pay fall into two categories. There are those which you have to pay and those which you would like to pay. Those which you would like to pay are called discretionary costs in that you would only pay them if you have any money spare and they are not necessary at that time. You will have to pay, say, £500 for food and other necessities leaving £200 spare for non-necessities.

Where is the control exercised here?

The answer is that the control over the bank is done by 'flexing' the discretionary payments to ensure that we stay in credit in the bank.

It is exactly the same in a company situation.

We have an opening position which consists of three known figures:

1. Opening Bank Balance

2. Opening Accounts Receivable

3. Opening Accounts Payable

These are the three monetary items which we know reasonably well will come to pass. We then need to superimpose the projected monthly receipts and payments onto this opening position to arrive at the projected monthly bank balance.

**Broad Background**

Cash itself is a commodity which is required to run a business and it should be treated like any other resource. There needs to be an adequate flow of cash and liquidity in the company for it to survive and the profitability of the company is one way to achieve this but of course money can come from outside such as from shareholders or banks.

The main reasons for producing a cash flow forecast are to ascertain whether:

a) Some action is needed to acquire further cash to ensure the company's financial plans are carried out, or,

b) There could be a surplus of cash and this could be invested more profitably than just sitting in the bank account.

Cash budgeting itself is of little use without action to follow it up and usually a cash budget is drawn up twice. The first time is to see what the cash flow would be without certain actions being taken. The second time is to incorporate the results of those actions in the final cash budget.

Benefits of a cash budget

1. Action can be taken to alleviate problems or re-invest spare cash.

2. Sometimes a seemingly good plan falls apart financially when the cash flow is examined. Action can be taken in advance.

3. It is a good communication tool for non-financial staff.

4. The act of producing the cash budget, as with all budgets, makes for deeper thought.

5. Variances in cash flow can be examined and justified.

Major factors for consideration

Time Scale: Short term budgets incorporate more detail and the more pressing the cash flow problems the shorter the term of the forecasting.

Classification of Costs: The split of fixed and variable costs and discretionary and non-discretionary costs is important for when the forecast needs adjusting for changes in activity levels.

Accuracy of Forecasts: The accuracy of the forecasts is critical to management decisions and the degree of accuracy in the estimations should be clearly stated and 'sensitivity analysis' applied where there are critical assumptions made. (Sensitivity analysis is the testing of changes in different underlying assumptions)

**Technical Aspects**

Step 1 - opening position

The first step is to establish the dates at which the cash flow is to commence and cease and the opening position of the bank, debtors and creditors. This will give us much of the initial cash flow in the first two months with the addition of non-credit items such as wages.

Step 2 - A budgeted monthly profit projection should then be created based upon all the other budgets created such as sales, production, labour etc.

Step 3 - cash projection

The cash flow forecast is then created from the information on the profit forecast making allowance for no depreciation, credit periods and capital items.

The following should be noted:

- The opening and closing bank are put together at the foot of the forecast with an extra line added for the monthly cash flow. This line is the difference between the receipts and payments for the month and does, of course, automatically highlight the good and bad months.

- Other receipts might be share issues, loans received, refunds or sale of assets.

- Wages are usually assumed no credit (although deducted tax is paid the following month).

- Remember that items go in the profit forecast as they are incurred. They go in the cash flow when they are paid.

- Purchase of Non-Current Assets go in the cash flow but not in the profit forecast. Depreciation would be in the profit forecast but not in the cash flow.

- Loan interest is in the profit forecast but the interest and the loan repayment would go in the cash flow.

- The Totals across and down should be extracted as they prove the additions before we show the effect on the bank at the bottom.

## Step 4 - interpretation

The figures are then examined with particular reference to the bank 'facility'. The facility is what we are allowed to borrow up to and this figure should always be in our mind during the preparation of the cash flow forecast.

If the facility was breeched, then action would need to be taken such as delaying payment to accounts payable, speeding up payments from accounts receivable or raising extra finance.

In general we need to establish what the cause of the problem is before we take remedial action. If the problem is lack of short term funds (working capital) to pay basic bills then we must have a working capital solution. i.e. the strategy is to improve our collection of debts, pay our bills slower, reduce the inventories or raise the bank facility. If the problem is caused by the purchase of a non-current asset then this is a long term asset and should be funded by long term finance such as a bank loan, leasing or share issue. Alternatively, we delay the purchase or arrange extended credit. What we do not do is use short term finance (bank current a/c) to fund long term assets.

## Appendix 8 – CAPEX Decisions - Capital Investment Appraisal

## What is investment appraisal?

In general, a company has to commit a great deal of capital to a project without getting an immediate return from the 'investment'. It is therefore necessary to have some way of determining firstly whether an investment is worthwhile or feasible on its own and secondly if there is a choice of two or more projects, which is the best one.

The former is determined essentially by whether the total money invested in the project is recovered during the life of the project. The latter is determined by a series of 'ranking' methods depending on which appraisal technique is chosen.

## Steps in Investment Appraisal

- The total project requirements need to be ascertained over the relevant number of years. For instance, a corner shop might only be looking over a 6 month period and a large multi-national corporation might be looking over a 5-10 year period.

- The sum total of all the possible projects is then computed over the time period and it is then compared with the available capital. Most often there is a shortfall as the capital is restricted or 'rationed' for a whole variety of reasons.

E.g. Desire of business owner to stay within a certain size, shortage of cash, inability to raise the finance from the bank or shareholders, caution, decision to invest only out of the previous year's profits.

- The projects then have to be ranked alongside each other to establish which gives the best rate of return.

Strangely, it is not always the project which gives the highest return which is approved. When a sum of money is set aside for investing in capital projects, one large project might use less of that sum of money than two small projects. For instance, suppose there was £100,000 available to be spent on capital projects and there are three possible projects all independent of one another (i.e. pursuing one project does not invalidate any of the others):

Project 1 costs £80,000 and yields 12% per annum.

Project 2 costs £60,000 and yields 11% per annum

Project 3 costs £40,000 and yields 10% per annum.

We also assume any spare capital not used is invested at 4%.

On the face of it Project 1 is the most lucrative as this will net 12% or £9,600 per annum plus give 4% on the remaining £20,000 i.e. £800. Total **£10,400**

However, if we select project two we also have enough capital left to also select project three. We would therefore earn as follows:

Project 2 - 11% of £60,000 = £6,600, Project 3 - 10% of £40,000 = £4,000 giving a total of **£10,600** which gives a better overall return on the capital.

This is relevant for independent 'projects' but projects can also be 'mutually exclusive'. Here, the acceptance of one project immediately excludes the commencement of another. For instance, the purchase of an I.T. system where one might be looking to purchase only one system out of a choice of three suppliers.

A method is therefore needed to rank projects against each other and the following techniques are the most common.

## Techniques

- Payback

- Return on Investment

- Accounting Rate of Return

- Discounted Cash Flow – Net Present Value or Internal Rate of Return

## Payback

This method assesses how quickly the capital outlay is recouped from the project.

For instance, you wish to purchase a machine costing £8,000 and it will save you £2,000 per annum in reduced wastage. The capital should be divided by the annual savings to get the payback. In this case it is 4 yrs.

We should normally talk about the 'cash flows' generated by a project rather than the profit as we are looking at the real payback of cash and not an accounting concept such as profit. This therefore means when assessing the running costs of the machine that we should ignore depreciation as the cash flow is unaffected by it. Note also in assessing cash flows from a project, they can be savings made as well as revenue created.

Alternatively, the cash flows from a project may be uneven in which case a cumulative approach to the cash flows should be adopted. In other words, add up the cash flows until the capital outlay is reached taking the initial capital outlay being in Year 0.

Example

A project needs £16,000 capital and its cash flows are:

|        | Cash Flows | Cumul CFs |
|--------|-----------|-----------|
| Year 0 | (16,000)  | (16,000)  |
| Year 1 | 5,000     | (11,000)  |
| Year 2 | 6,000     | (5,000)   |
| Year 3 | 4,000     | (1,000)   |
| Year 4 | 4,000     | 3,000     |

Its payback is clearly during year 4. The payback is year 3 plus an extra £1,000 needed from year 4. We assume that the cash flows are even during the year and therefore it is £1,000 out of £4,000 (year 4 cash flow) from year 4 or £1,000 ÷ £4,000 = ¼ of the year so payback is 3 years 3 months.

The shorter the time period of returning the initial outlay, the less risk there is. Not only is the capital at risk for less time but also our ability to predict benefits in the future significantly decreases the further into the future we go.

This is undoubtedly the most commonly used form of appraisal mainly because it is the easiest for everyone to understand with limited training. It does have its weaknesses and one is that it does not assess the return after the payback period. However, many large companies use payback on the basis that provided there is a return after the payback period then that is often so far into the future that provided the money has been paid back quickly all the rest is a bonus. It is not sophisticated but it does work. The most common use is as a 'hurdle rate' such as 'we shall not consider any project which gives less than a three year payback'. This has the effect of whittling down the number of projects and then another more complex form of appraisal is used alongside.

- When companies reach a cash flow problem, they will often set the minimum payback period as low as two years or even one year!

- In order to rank a project with this method, one clearly chooses the one with the quickest payback.

**Return on Investment**

This method is very simple and not commonly used but it helps to explain the following slightly more complex method of ARR.

It is quite simply, a calculation of the average annual return from a project during its life that is assessed against the capital outlay. It is therefore very like looking at the return from a building society or bank over several years.

For instance, a capital outlay of £21,000 yields cash flows of £10,000, £5,000, £8,000, £5,000 over its 4 year life. Total cash flows are £28,000 or £7,000 per year.

£7,000 as a % of £21,000 gives 33.3%, which may be compared with another project and the one with the highest return is picked.

There is one main problem with this method:

No allowance is made for the value of the equipment (investment) at the end of the project. It cannot be compared therefore with the cost of the source of capital.

This helps to explain the next more commonly used method of appraisal.

**Accounting Rate of Return (ARR)**

In the example above, we assume that the initial investment is written down to nothing by the end of the project period. This therefore means we can get at the 'average' capital employed in the project. If the capital outlay is £21,000 at the beginning and it is worthless after 4 years, the average capital tied up is the opening capital of £21,000 plus the closing value of zero divided by two. i.e. £10,500. We also recalculate the project cash flow to allow for a write off of the equipment over its life. The cash flows are a total of £28,000 but after writing off the equipment/capital cost of £21,000, we are left with £7,000 or £1,750 per annum.

We now have an **ARR** calculation as follows:

Net cash Flow p.a. (after deducting capital) ÷ Average Capital Employed X 100

£1,750 ÷ £10,500 X 100 = 16.7%

This can be used to compare both with other project returns and also with the cost of the source of capital so provided we provide capital at a cost which is less than 16.7%, the project is feasible.

There is one final drawback to this method of appraisal and that is that it makes no allowance for the time value of money as discussed in the next section on discounted cash flow.

**Discounted Cash Flow – Net Present Value Method (NPV)**

This method has become increasingly popular in the last 20 years not least because of the development of IT industry software. As it is more complex, it requires a great many calculations that are, of course, easily done with a spreadsheet. The basic principle is that when we expend money today and try to relate it to money received in several years' time then we are comparing 'unlike' units. For instance, would you rather receive £1,000 today or in one year's time? If you receive £1,000 now you could invest it at, say, 10% and it is worth £1,100 in a year. This therefore means that £1,100 received in one year has a 'present value' of £1,000. £1,000 received today would be worth £1,210 in two years' time (compound interest of 10%). So the present value of £1,210 received in 2 years is £1,000, and so on.

In order to judge one project against another, we can use a ranking method called the profitability index (PI).
Whereas the NPV = Present Values – Cost
The PI = Present Values ÷ Cost

To be viable, a project must have a PI greater than or equal to 1.
An alternative method of ranking is to calculate the NPV per £1 of Capital.

Both methods are used to rank but difficulties come where the capital payments are spread. In this case, all the capital outlay which is not in the first year needs to be converted to present value. Lengthening the capital payments like shortening the cash flow time period would make a project more viable.

Due to this problem, many companies often rank by the highest NPV rather than the highest NPV per £1 of capital which would result in a more efficient use of capital. The problem is then extended into what is capital and what is revenue in a project!

If the NPV works out at exactly zero, this means that the project is yielding exactly the same as the rate of the borrowed money. So if a discount rate was used in a project of, say, 12% and it gives an NPV of zero, this 12% would be the Internal rate of Return (IRR). This is the effective rate that the project is yielding and is dealt with next.

**Internal Rate of Return**

The internal rate of return is the rate of return that a project is yielding. It can be arrived at by an iterative process of constantly changing the discount rate until the NPV comes to zero. The benefit of also calculating the IRR is that you get an idea about how far above the cost of capital the project is and so it gives some idea as to the riskiness of the project being unprofitable. Needless to say a spreadsheet formula can calculate the IRR instantly as for the NPV so long drawn out calculations are not necessary.

There is a method for calculating the IRR that revolves around making two guesses and interpolating between them.

This consists of taking a best guess at what the IRR might be. The NPV calculation is then worked out and if the result is a surplus then this means that the IRR must be higher than the first guess. A second guess is then made of a much higher rate in order to calculate an NPV which is negative. This will then prove that the IRR is between the two guesses. It is necessary to have two guesses which span the real rate.

Now the formula can be applied:

IRR = A + (a ÷ (a-b) × (B-A)

Where 'A' is the guess of the lower interest rate. 'a' is the surplus from applying the lower rate A. 'b' is the deficiency from the higher interest rate applied. '(a-b)' is the spread of the surplus and deficiency from the two rates. i.e. if there was a surplus of +3,500 on guess 1 and a deficiency of -1,200 on guess 2, '(a-b)' would be 4,700. 'B-A' is the difference between the interest rates – if guess 1 was 7% and guess 2 was 12%, 'B-A' would be 5% (12%-7%).

Example

Calculate the IRR of a project for a company with capital outlay of £7,500 and cash flows over 5 years of £2,000 per year.

Step 1 – NPV of two guesses

First guess of, say, 5% discount rate gives NPV of £1,159

Second guess of, say, 14% discount rate gives NPV of -£633.84

Step 2 – Apply Formula

IRR = A + (a ÷ (a-b) × (B-A)

   = 5% + (1,159 ÷ (1,159 + 633.84) × (14%-5%)

   = 5% + .646 × 9%

   = 10.82% (Note the actual Excel formula answer is 10.4%)

The accuracy is increased if there is a narrow spread of interest rates and also the rate calculated should always be tested to produce close to zero in an NPV calculation as where there are large tranches of capital investment producing a mixture of positive and negative cash flows, some odd results can follow giving a mathematical possibility of more than one rate!

It is a useful tool to have alongside an NPV calculation as it gives a percentage return as well as an absolute one. It will usually produce the same decision as NPV unless there are projects of very different magnitude. For instance, it is quite possible to have an IRR of 20% on a small project with an NPV of, say, £30,000. Compare this with a larger project with an IRR of 18% but an NPV of £40,000.

## Discounted Payback

This is a hybrid of DCF and payback and simply means how long does it take to get the initial capital back **after** discounting the cash flows against the cost of capital. It is basically a more refined version of payback which makes allowance for the time value of money.

## Cost of Capital

If you borrow money and a half is a bank loan @ 6% and the other half is a loan @ 10% then the Average Cost of Capital is (10% + 6%) ÷ 2 = 8%

However, capital in a company is made up of several elements such as Ordinary Shares, Preference Shares, Bank Loans and Overdraft, all with differing proportions.

Each element has a cost. With a bank it is the interest but what about the Ordinary Shares (Equity). Do they really have a cost as we only normally pay a dividend when we make a profit and even then we are not committed to paying it?

The cost of equity is twofold. Firstly, we are offering growth in share price and if we do not give that in the long term as a quoted company we will cease to exist. Secondly we are offering a dividend with growth which is also a long term commitment to the shareholders even though it is not a contractual one.

The capital in a company therefore has a cost overall as well as in its different parts. The overall cost is known as the Weighted Average Cost of Capital (WACC) and the cost of an individual part of capital used for a project is known as the 'Marginal' cost of capital.

Suppose a company had the following capital structure, Share Capital of £60,000 which paid a 4% dividend yield and offered growth of 10% and £40,000 loans at a bank rate of 6%, what would be the WACC?

|        | Capital | Cost | Weighted Cost |
|--------|---------|------|---------------|
| Equity | 60,000  | 14%  | 8,400         |
| Loans  | 40,000  | 6%   | 2,400         |
| Totals | 100,000 |      | 10,800        |

Therefore WACC calculation is 10,800 ÷ 100,000 × 100 = 10.8%

(*note that the cost of the Equity of 14% is 10% growth plus 4% dividend yield)

Suppose the capital moved to £40,000 Equity and £60,000 loans, it would be calculated as follows:

|        | Capital | Cost | Weighted Cost |
|--------|---------|------|---------------|
| Equity | 40,000  | 14%  | 5,600         |
| Loans  | 60,000  | 6%   | 3,600         |
| Totals | 100,000 |      | 9,200         |

Therefore WACC calculation is now 9,200 ÷ 100,000 × 100 = 9.2%

One might think that there is no point having expensive Equity if loans are so much cheaper in the long run but high loans severely increases the financial risk of the organisation.

For smaller capital purchases, the marginal cost would often be used unless the project is so big that it will alter the capital structure in the company, in which case either the new WACC should be calculated or the old WACC if there is a commitment to retain the same capital structure. In other words, if the WACC is 12% but we are raising £2,000,000 by 8% bank loans to put into a project (eg a takeover), the company may well have taken its gearing above an acceptable level and would rectify this by an issue of shares after the takeover thus retaining the WACC at its former level.

## Appendix 9 - Taxation Notes

Payroll Tax, Corporation Tax and Value Added Tax

Payroll Tax

If a company employs people then it will almost certainly have to deduct income tax and national insurance from their wages. The amount of income tax varies from individual to individual and depends on how much they earn.  HMRC issues each individual with a code based upon their personal circumstances, which is copied to the employer who can then calculate how much tax to deduct as directed by HMRC.

National Insurance (NI) is also based upon earnings and is in two parts. There is NI deducted from the employee's earnings and there is a separate proportion of NI that the employer has to pay.

The employer pays the tax/national insurance to HMRC on the 19th of the month after it has been deducted together with the employer's portion of the NI.

An example for a monthly paid employee for June would be as follows:

| Gross Wages for month | | 800 |
|---|---|---|
| Less Deductions | | |
| Taxation | 93 | |
| Employee's NI | 56 | (149) |
| Net Wages paid to employee | £ | 651 |
| | | |
| Payment to HMRC | | |
| Taxation | | 93 |
| Employee's NI | 56 | |
| Employer's NI | 87 | 143 |
| Payment sent to HMRC | £ | 236 |

The employee receives £651 on 30th June and HMRC receives £236 by the 19th of July. Two important issues are worth noting. The cost of employing this person is not £800 per month but £800 + the employer's NI of £87 = £887 and this should be reflected in the costs of an employee e.g. when costing a product. The second point is that the cash flow is affected in that net wages are paid in June but HMRC is paid in July.

## Corporation/Income Tax

Limited companies pay corporation tax on their profits (23% but falling to 20% by 2015) and sole traders and partners pay income tax again on their profits (rates between 10% and 45% - basic rate currently 20%). These taxes are payable the year following the production of the financial accounts for a year's trading.

## Value Added Tax (sales tax)

When businesses sales are over £79,000 p.a. they must, with some exceptions, add VAT on to the price of the goods they are selling. They usually have to add 20% but there are some variations.

They pay this VAT over to HMRC every 3 months (although they can elect to pay monthly) and they are allowed to deduct any VAT they have paid from the amount they pay HMRC.

e.g. If I am charged £400 for materials then I will be invoiced for £400 plus 20% VAT = £480

If I then sell the materials for £1,000, I will have to add on a further (20%) £200 for VAT, ie I will charge my customer £1,200.

I will have made £600 (£1000 - £400) profit and I will have to pay £120 (£200 - £80) to HMRC.

If a bill from a customer includes VAT such as a restaurant bill, then the vat element is calculated by multiplying by 20 ÷ 120 = 1/6

Example to calculate the vat element of a bill for £1,200

1/6 x £1,200 = £200 so the net sales would be £1,000 and the VAT (20%) would be £200

Implications – Broadly speaking, VAT builds up over the 3 months and is then generally self-cancelling until goods are retailed where HMRC makes its money. It can severely affect cash flow exaggerating the peaks and troughs and causes significant book-keeping headaches for the smaller businesses. (Imagine purchasing a machine for £100,000, you would pay £120,000 and not get the £20,000 VAT back from HMRC for perhaps 3 months!) VAT does not show in the Income Statement figures but will show in the Balance Sheet where sums are outstanding as either a creditor or a debtor depending on the type of business involved. See http://www.hmrc.gov.uk/vat.

# 18. Appendices Part 2 - Questions

## Chapter 2

Q.1 Calculate the gross profit from the following: Closing Inventory £27,000, Sales £70,000, Opening Inventory £17,000, Direct Wages £13,000, Purchases of Materials £47,000.

Q.2 Create an Income Statement from the following:

| | |
|---|---|
| Purchases | 43,300 |
| Direct Wages | 36,000 |
| Opening Inventory | 27,596 |
| Indirect Wages | 14,500 |
| Sales | 120,000 |
| Other overheads | 27,834 |
| Closing Inventory | 26,000 |

Q.3

The Sales for the year ended 31/03/2013 are £63,000 and Jim had incurred the following costs for the year:

| | £ |
|---|---|
| Cost of supplies | 42,000 |
| Purchase of machinery | 5,000 |
| Rent & Rates of warehouse | 4,300 |
| Electricity | 850 |
| Motor & travel Expenses | 2,600 |
| Sundry expenses | 750 |
| Advertising & Printing | 3,700 |
| Bank Interest payable | 1,200 |

He had also taken drawings for himself of £15,500 out of the business bank account during the year and had inventory left at the year-end of £6,500 value.

## Chapter 3

Q.1

What are the alternative names for the Matching concept?

Q.2 Year-end inventory should be valued at the lower of cost and net realisable value. Which concept is being applied here?

Q.3 Last year the finished goods part of the inventory was valued at selling price less 25%. This year it is valued at selling price less 20%. With which concept is this in conflict?

Q.4 Having purchased new machinery for £100,000, the owner valued them at the year end at £40,000 on the basis of what he would get if he tried to sell them on liquidation of the company. With which concept is this in conflict?

Q.5 The company year end is $30^{th}$ November and the rent paid quarterly in advance is as follows:

30 10 13 - £6,000

31 01 14 - £6,000

30 04 14 - £6,000

31 07 14 - £9,000

30 10 14 - £9,000

What should the rent be for the year ended 31/12/2014? How much is "prepaid" at the year end? What concept is being applied here?

Q.6 If you purchase a car for the business, is it a capital expense or an operating expense? Would this classification change if you were a car dealer?

Q.7 Which of the following are normally a capital expense? Rent, Machinery, bank interest, Leasehold improvements, wages of staff, electricity costs.

## Chapter 4

Q.1 What is the closing figure in the capital account after the following transactions? Drawings £2,500, Loss £3,000, Opening Capital £4,000.

Q.2 What is the profit for the year if the drawings are £3,500, Capital introduced was £1,000, the opening capital was £2,000 and the closing capital is £6,500?

Q.3 Which are the 5 major headings in a Balance Sheet?

Q.4 Create a Balance Sheet as at 31.3 2014 for the following:

Q.4

| | |
|---|---|
| Machinery | 7,500 |
| Accounts Payable | 5,350 |
| Accounts Receivable | 4,385 |
| Inventories | 7,250 |
| Bank Balance in Credit | 4,320 |
| Profit in Year | 9,850 |
| Loans | 6,750 |
| Opening Capital | 3,000 |
| Drawings | 4,000 |
| VAT Due (Sales Tax) | 2,505 |

# Chapter 5

## Q.1

Using the following figures, calculate the depreciation and net book values for 6 years using both the Straight Line and Reducing Balance (25%) methods:

Initial cost of a car is £24,000. It is expected to be worth £6,000 when sold in 6 years time.

# Chapter 6

Q.1 Show the cash book entries for the following transactions and also the closing balance: Money received from customers £3,100, money paid to suppliers £6,250, Opening bank balance (overdrawn) £2,500.

Q.2 Show the effect including any relevant figure from Q.1 above on the sales ledger if the opening balance of what customers owe is £2,700 and the sales invoiced are £8,000.

# Chapter 7

## Q.1

Calculate the Equity Value at the year ended 31.12.14 from the following figures:

Ordinary Share Capital (1.1.14) £25,000, Dividends paid in Year £13,800, Interest paid £17,000, Operating Profit (PBIT) £55,000, Corporation Tax £9,000, Opening Retained Profits (1.1.2014) £10,000,

## Q.2

Calculate the Balance Sheet value of one share from the following figures:

Share Capital 400,000 Ordinary Shares of £0.40 each, retained profits at 1.1.2014 £240,000, Profit for the year ended 31.12.14 £95,000, Dividends in year £15,000.

Chapter 8

Q.1

Interpret the proceeding figures for Blaster Ltd using the following ratios and previous year figures:

| RATIOS | Previous |
|---|---|
| Profitability | Year |
| Return on Capital Employed (%) | 34 % |
| Return on Sales (%) | 18 % |
| Gross Margin (%) | 56 % |
| | |
| Financial Status | |
| Current | 2.0 |
| Acid Test (Quick Ratio) | 1.4 |
| Gearing (accountants) % | 48 % |
| | |
| Activity (Efficiency) Ratios | |
| Inventory Days | 110 |
| Accounts Receivable (Debtors) | 60 |
| Accounts Payable (Creditors) | 47 |

# Blaster Ltd

| Q.1 | | | | | | | |
|---|---|---|---|---|---|---|---|
| **Income Statement** | | | | **Balance Sheet** | | | |
| A | B | C | D | E | F | G | |
| Sales | | 360,000 | | **ASSETS** | | | 3 |
| Less Cost of Sales | | | | Non-Current Assets | | | 4 |
| Opening Inventory | 37,600 | | | Machinery (after dep'n to date) | 66,000 | | 5 |
| Add Purchases | 212,700 | | | Less Depreciation for year | (16,000) | 50,000 | 6 |
| | 250,300 | | | Current Assets | | | 7 |
| Less Closing Inventory | (67,200) | | | Inventories | 45,700 | | 8 |
| Cost of Sales | | (183,100) | | Accounts Receivable | 75,000 | | 9 |
| **Gross Profit** | | 176,900 | | Bank Balance | 27,700 | | 10 |
| **Less Expenses** | | | | | | 148,400 | 11 |
| Indirect Wages | 76,300 | | | Total Assets | | 198,400 | 12 |
| Marketing Costs | 25,600 | | | | | | 13 |
| Depreciation | 16,000 | | | **EQUITY & LIABILITIES** | | | 14 |
| Other overheads | 14,000 | (131,900) | | Equity | | | 15 |
| **Operating Profit (PBIT)** | | 45,000 | | Share Capital | 16,500 | | 16 |
| Less Bank Interest Paid | | (7,200) | | Retained Profits (inc. current) | 65,240 | | 17 |
| Profit Before Tax | | 37,800 | | | 81,740 | | 18 |
| Corporation Tax Due | | (7,560) | | Dividend | (14,000) | | 19 |
| Profit After Tax | | 30,240 | | Equity Value | | 67,740 | 20 |
| | | | | Non Current Liabilities - Loans | | 86,400 | 21 |
| | | | | Current Liabilities | | | 22 |
| | | | | Accounts Payable | 36,700 | | 23 |
| | | | | Corporation Tax Due | 7,560 | | 24 |
| | | | | | | 44,260 | 25 |
| | | | | | | | 26 |
| | | | | Total Equity & Liabilities | | 198,400 | 27 |

# Q.2

Interpret the proceeding figures for Claxton Ltd using the following ratios and previous year figures:

| RATIOS | Previous Year |
|---|---|
| **Profitability** | |
| Return on Capital Employed (%) | 71 % |
| Return on Sales (%) | 20 % |
| Gross Margin (%) | 61 % |
| | |
| **Financial Status** | |
| Current | 2.3 |
| Acid Test (Quick Ratio) | 1.1 |
| Gearing (accountants) % | 46 % |
| | |
| **Activity (Efficiency) Ratios** | |
| Inventory Days | 222 |
| Accounts Receivable (Debtors) | 76 |
| Accounts Payable (Creditors) | 30 |

# Claxton Ltd

| Q.2 | | | | | | | |
|---|---|---|---|---|---|---|---|
| Income Statement | | | | Balance Sheet | | | |
| A | B | C | D | E | F | G | |
| Sales | | 240,000 | | **ASSETS** | | | 3 |
| Less Cost of Sales | | | | Non-Current Assets | | | 4 |
| Opening Inventory | 4,200 | | | Car | 12,000 | | 5 |
| Add Purchases | 147,000 | | | Less Depreciation | (4,000) | 8,000 | 6 |
| | 151,200 | | | Current Assets | | | 7 |
| Less Closing Inventory | (57,200) | | | Inventories | 57,200 | | 8 |
| Cost of Sales | | (94,000) | | Accounts Receivable | 50,300 | | 9 |
| **Gross Profit** | | 146,000 | | | | 107,500 | 10 |
| **Less Expenses** | | | | Total Assets | | 115,500 | 11 |
| Indirect Wages | 35,400 | | | | | | 12 |
| Director & Sec Salaries | 25,600 | | | **EQUITY & LIABILITIES** | | | 13 |
| Depreciation | 4,000 | | | Equity | | | 14 |
| Other overheads | 32,400 | (97,400) | | Share Capital | 10,000 | | 15 |
| **Operating Profit (PBIT)** | | 48,600 | | Profit in Year | 32,900 | | 16 |
| Less Bank Interest Paid | | (7,200) | | | 42,900 | | 17 |
| Profit Before Tax | | 41,400 | | Dividend | (6,000) | | 18 |
| Corporation Tax Due | | (8,500) | | Equity Value | | 36,900 | 19 |
| Profit After Tax | | 32,900 | | Non Current Liabilities - Loans | | 31,800 | 20 |
| | | | | Current Liabilities | | | 21 |
| | | | | Accounts Payable | 12,000 | | 22 |
| | | | | Corporation Tax Due | 8,500 | | 23 |
| | | | | Bank Overdraft | 26,300 | | 24 |
| | | | | | | 46,800 | 25 |
| | | | | | | | 26 |
| | | | | Total Equity & Liabilities | | 115,500 | 27 |

# Chapter 9

## Q.1

From the Income Statement, the Profit for the year is £75,000

Balance Sheet in £'000s

| | Year 1 | Year 2 |
|---|---|---|
| Non-Current Assets | 600 | 1000 |
| Depreciation | | (50) |
| | 600 | 950 |
| Inventories | 325 | 190 |
| Accounts Receivable | 200 | 150 |
| Bank | 200 | 255 |
| | 1325 | 1545 |
| Accounts Payable | 400 | 450 |
| Loans | 400 | 470 |
| Shares | 100 | 125 |
| Reserves | 425 | 500 |
| | 1325 | 1545 |

Show the sources and uses of funds over the two years linking the profit to the movement in the bank.

## Q.2

Interpret the following Statement of Cash Flows:

|  | £ | £ |
|---|---|---|
| Operating Profit for period |  | 50,000 |
| Add Depreciation |  | 10,000 |
| Adjusted Profit |  | 60,000 |
| Change in receivables | (20,000) |  |
| Change in payables | (35,000) |  |
| Change in inventories | 4,000 |  |
| Interest Paid | (10,000) |  |
| Tax Paid | (15,000) | (76,000) |
| **Cash Flow from Operating Activities** |  | (16,000) |
|  |  |  |
| Sale of Subsidiary | 85,500 |  |
| Purchase of Machinery | (30,700) |  |
| **Cash Flow from Investing Activities** |  | 54,800 |
|  |  |  |
| Issue of Shares | 20,000 |  |
| Loans Repaid | (35,000) |  |
| Dividends Paid | (17,500) |  |
| Cash Flow from Financing Activites |  | (32,500) |
|  |  |  |
| Change in Cash over the period |  | 6,300 |
| Cash at beginning of year |  | (49,700) |
| Cash at end of year |  | (43,400) |

## Chapter 11

### Q.1

A company makes one product in batches (weighing 45 kilos) of 12. Calculate the costs of one unit of product with the following information:

Materials needed for a batch - Material A 30 kilograms @ £2.50 per kilo. Material B 15 kilograms @ £3.00 per kilo. However, there will be 5 kilos wastage so 20 kilograms will be needed.

Labour needed for a batch - 15 hours @ £12 per hour.

The overheads for the month are £75,000 and the company budget on 600 batches per month.

### Q.2

#### Part 1

You are required to allocate costs to the two departments.

The budgeted overheads for the period are made up as follows:

| | |
|---|---|
| Manufacturing consumables | 4,000 |
| Assembly consumables | 6,000 |
| Supervisory wages | 45,000 |
| Canteen costs | 18,000 |
| Rent Costs | 30,000 |
| Machinery Maintenance | 12,000 |
| Heating & Lighting | 18,000 |
| Total Overheads | £133,000 |

You also have the following departmental information:

|  | Manufacturing | Assembly | Totals |
|---|---|---|---|
| Number of Staff | 10 | 40 | 50 |
| Value of Machinery | £40,000 | £20,000 | £60,000 |
| Area occupied | 1,500 m$^2$ | 3,000 m$^2$ | 4,500 m$^2$ |

Part 2

Now suppose manufacturing recovered its overheads based on machine hours and its budgeted machine hours for the period were 500 and Assembly recovered its overheads based on labour hours and its budgeted labour hours for the period were 1,500, calculate the overhead recovery rates for each department.

Part 3

What would be the total cost of a product with materials of £500, labour 4 hours @ £20/hour and machine hours of 2? (Hint – separate the machine overheads from the assembly overheads)

Q.3

A business has 2 products and recovers its overheads in proportion to its direct costs.  Teddy Bears and Dolls. Last month the business produced 2,000 Teddy Bears and 1,500 Dolls.  The Teddy Bears used £14,000 of direct costs and the Dolls used £6,000 of direct costs. The overheads last month were £6,600.

What were the total costs per unit of each product?

# Chapter 12

## Q.1

Jim is putting on a rock festival and has a choice venue, acts, security etc. From the following two situations, calculate the break-even number of tickets to be sold, the budgeted profit and the margin of safety.

### Situation 1

Cost of rock groups £2.5 million. Cost of land rent, security etc. £1.5 million. The tickets would sell for £220 each and the estimated cost of supplying food, tent accommodation etc. would be £80 per person. The budgeted sales of tickets are expected to be about 35,000.

### Situation 2

Cost of rock groups £2.0 million. Cost of land rent, security etc £1.5 million. The tickets would sell for £100 each and the estimated variable costs of 10% of the ticket price (no supplying of food, tent accommodation etc.) per person. The budgeted sales of tickets are expected to be about 50,000.

Which would be the better proposition?

## Q.2

Gotham City Council had a severe shortage of Batmobiles (due to Robin's Saturday night drunken revelries) and have placed an initial order with Joker Fabrications Ltd for 10 new Batmobiles at a price of £4,000 each.

a) Calculate the profit for Joker Fabrications Ltd on this order given that the fixed costs are £21,600 and the variable costs are 40% of the sales. They have no other orders.

b) Calculate the break-even number of Batmobiles and the maximum profit achievable given an overall plant capacity of 15 Units.

c) If the sales price of the contract for the 10 Batmobiles is fixed, to what percentage must the variable costs be reduced in order to give a 10% return on sales?

Q.3

|  | Totals | T-Shirts | Jumpers | Jeans |
|---|---|---|---|---|
| Sales | 90,000 | 51,000 | 21,000 | 18,000 |
| Total Costs | 73,750 | 38,250 | 15,750 | 19,750 |
| Profit | 16,250 | 12,750 | 5,250 | (1,750) |

You ascertain that the fixed costs for each product are 2/3rds of the total costs. The owner of the business suggests eliminating the Jeans line. Is he wise? What are the other commercial issues?

Q.4

Scarce Resources - SCREAMING ABDABS

The Screaming Abdabs Alarm Co Ltd. sells three models of alarms and needs to establish the most profitable mix of sales across the three products for the month as there is a dock strike estimated to cause a shortage of bells (which are imported) for the alarms for one month only.

The 'Shrieker' model utilises 3 bells and has potential sales of 6,000 units.

The 'Ear Splitter' model utilises 4 bells and has potential sales of 2,000 units.

The 'Nerve Buster' model utilises 5 bells and has potential sales of 3,000 units.

There are only 28,000 bells available in stock until the next estimated delivery.

Given that the fixed costs are £250,000 for the month, Optimise the product mix and calculate the most profit achievable given the following:

Shrieker has a selling price of £60 and variable costs of £30 per unit.

Ear Splitter has a selling price of £104 and variable costs of £56 per unit.

Nerve buster has a selling price of £130 and variable costs of £85 per unit.

Q.5

Monster Makers Ltd are having problems in drawing up their budgets for next year and have asked you to answer some questions after allowing for the following information.

They reconstruct human bodies from spare parts dug up when the moon is full.

Their supplies of corpses come from Burke & Hare Ltd at a cost of £1,000 each. (Paid in cash, of course!)

Their employees are all sub-contract being down and outs recruited from all the bars and bordellos in the region and are each paid £40 per day to re-assemble a complete corpse from good parts. They work a five-day week and it takes one week per employee to assemble one corpse.

The newly constructed bodies sell for £2,000 each to credit card companies who train them as customer services managers.

Monster Makers Ltd have fixed costs of £56,000 for the year.

a) What is the capacity of Monster Makers Ltd (in units and value) if their break-even is 40% of their capacity? What is therefore their maximum profit?

b) How many employees working full time are needed to achieve capacity if they work an effective 35-week year?

c) To accommodate an increase in fixed costs of £32,000 for consultancy fees for Baron Frankenstein, how many extra units above current capacity need to be sold to also give the Baron a return on his capital invested (£100,000 to increase the capacity) of 20%.

d) Draw a break-even chart. See appendix 5.

# Chapter 13

## Q.1

Calculate and explain the variances and describe the weaknesses in this 'fixed' budget:

|  | Budget | Actual |
|---|---|---|
|  | £ | £ |
| Sales | 21,000 | 20,400 |
| Direct Materials | 8,400 | 9,000 |
| Direct Labour | 6,500 | 5,300 |
| Variable Overhead | 3,000 | 2,900 |
| Fixed Overhead | 2,200 | 2,400 |
| Profit | 900 | 800 |

## Q.2

Decompose the following costs into fixed, variable and semi-variable:

| Units | 3,000 | 4,000 |
|---|---|---|
| Materials | 15,000 | 20,000 |
| Rent | 7,000 | 7,000 |
| Telephone | 6,000 | 7,500 |

What would be the budget for each cost at activity level of 7,000 units?

## Q.3

Grimsby Borough Council's municipal baths operates a restaurant for which the following budget report has been prepared. Rewrite it in a more useful form to management (i.e. flexed budget) as the manager has been castigated for going over budget on all his expenses.

|                    | y/e 31st March 2014 | | |
|                    | Budget | Actual | Variance |
| Number of Meals    | 36,000 | 43,200 | |
| Expenditure        | £ | £ | £ |
| Provisions         | 64,800 | 74,300 | -9,500 |
| Labour             | | | |
| - Supervisor       | 20,000 | 20,500 | -500 |
| - Staff            | 50,000 | 51,400 | -1,400 |
| Heat & Light       | 5,000 | 6,000 | -1,000 |
| Administration     | 8,600 | 10,100 | -1,500 |
| Total Exp.         | 148,400 | 162,300 | -13,900 |
| Income £4.30       | 154,800 | 185,760 | 30,960 |
| Surplus            | 6,400 | 23,460 | 17,060 |

Notes

- Supervisor's salary is a fixed cost. There are four catering staff each budgeted to cost £8,000 p.a. plus a rate based on the number of meals sold.
- Heat & light are a fixed cost.
- Admin costs are semi-variable with a fixed element amounting to £5,000.
- Meals are always sold on an average price of £4.30

# Chapter 14

## Q.1

Hole in the Dosh Ltd. are projecting their future cash requirements from 31.12.0X and have the following information:-

1) Accounts receivable (Debtors) at 31.12.0X are £48,000 payable 25% within one month and the 75% balance within 2 months.

2) Accounts payable (Creditors) at 31.12.0X are £40,000 payable within one month.

3) Opening unreconciled bank balance is £20,000 overdrawn but there are unpresented cheques to suppliers of £20,000.

4) Sales from January run at £28,000 per month rising in April to £40,000 per month thereafter. 50% of sales are paid without credit and the remainder on 2 months credit.

5) Purchases run at 25% of the invoiced monthly sales payable in one month from invoice.

6) Overheads are £3,000 per month payable monthly as due.

7) Capital equipment is to be purchased in January for £30,000 on two months credit.

8) There is a government grant expected in during May of £15,000.

9) Wages are £10,000 per month for the first three months and rising thereafter to £12,000 per month.

10) Depreciation for the year is £15,000.

11) The overdraft facility is £55,000 and the bank wish to reduce this.

_**Present a case to the bank and suggest how to manage the cash.**_

# Chapter 15

## Q.1

Calculate the payback time from the following:

Capital cost £30,000, Net cash flows years 1-4 respectively £10,000, £12,000, £6,000 and £4,000.

## Q.2

Which is the best project using the Accounting Rate of Return method assuming the capital cost is fully written off by the end of the project?

| Q.2 | | Project 1 Cash Flows | Project 2 Cash Flows |
|---|---|---|---|
| Year | 0 | (37,000) | (23,000) |
| Year | 1 | 14,000 | 3,000 |
| Year | 2 | 19,000 | 7,000 |
| Year | 3 | 12,000 | 12,000 |
| Year | 4 | 10,000 | 15,000 |
| Year | 5 | 6,000 | |

Would the decision change if payback was applied also?

## Q.3

Apply the Net Present Value method to Q.2 cash flows based on a 12% cost of capital with the following discount factors:

| Year | 1 | 0.893 |
|---|---|---|
| Year | 2 | 0.797 |
| Year | 3 | 0.712 |
| Year | 4 | 0.636 |
| Year | 5 | 0.567 |

Compare the different results from the different methods.

Q.4

Calculate which company has the highest cost of capital from the following figures:

| A | Capital | Cost |
|---|---|---|
| Equity | 150,000 | 14% |
| Loans | 50,000 | 5% |

| B | Capital | Cost |
|---|---|---|
| Equity | 40,000 | 18% |
| Loans | 80,000 | 8% |

# 19. Appendices Part 2 - Answers

## Chapter 2

### Answer.1

|  |  | £ |
|---|---|---|
| Sales |  | 70,000 |
| Opening Inventory | 17,000 |  |
| Purchases | 47,000 |  |
|  | 64,000 |  |
| Less Closing Inventory | 27,000 |  |
|  | 37,000 |  |
| Direct Wages | 13,000 |  |
| Cost of Sales |  | 50,000 |
| Gross Profit |  | 20,000 |

### Answer. 2

|  | £ | £ |
|---|---|---|
| Sales |  | 120,000 |
| Less Cost of Sales |  |  |
| Opening Inventory | 27,596 |  |
| Add Purchases | 43,300 |  |
|  | 70,896 |  |
| Less Closing Inventory | (26,000) |  |
| Purchases consumed | 44,896 |  |
| Direct Wages | 36,000 |  |
| Cost of Sales |  | (80,896) |
| Gross Profit |  | 39,104 |
| Less Expenses |  |  |
| Indirect Wages | 14,500 |  |
| Other overheads | 27,834 | (42,334) |
| Net Profit before drawings |  | (3,230) |

Answer.3

|  | £ | £ |
|---|---|---|
| Sales | | 63,000 |
| Less Cost of Sales | | |
| Cost of Supplies (Purchases) | 42,000 | |
| Less Closing Inventory | (6,500) | |
| | | (28,800) |
| Gross Profit | | 34,200 |
| Less Overheads | | |
| Rent & Rates of warehouse | 4,300 | |
| Electricity | 850 | |
| Motor & travel Expenses | 2,600 | |
| Sundry expenses | 750 | |
| Advertising & Printing | 3,700 | |
| Bank Interest payable | 1,200 | |
| Total Overheads | | (7,080) |
| Net Profit | | 27,120 |
| Drawings (S/B on Balance Sheet) | | (15,500) |
| Surplus after Drawings | | 11,620 |

Note that the Machinery does not show on the Income Statement as it is a Capital Expense.

Chapter 3

A.1 Matching concept, apportionment concept, accruals concept

A.2 Prudence concept

A.3 Consistency concept

A.4 Going Concern

A.5 Matching concept. £28,000. (2/3 of first bill and 1/3 of final bill). The prepayment is £6,000. Accruals concept.

A.6 Capital expense. If a car dealer, you would classify it as stock and therefore an operating expense, or more strictly a 'cost of sale'.

A.7 Machinery and Leasehold improvements

Chapter 4

A.1 Closing Capital is (£1,500) – Opening Capital of £4,000 less Drawings £2,500 less Loss £3,000

A.2 Profit is £7,000. Opening capital £2,000 + Capital introduced £1,000 + profit less drawings of £3,500 = Closing capital of £6,500? (Profit = Closing capital less opening capital + drawings)

A.3 Non-current and Current Assets, Non-current and Current Liabilities and the Capital account.

## A.4 Balance Sheet as at 31.3 2014

| A.4 | Balance Sheet | |
|---|---|---|
| **ASSETS** | | |
| Non-Current Assets | | £ |
| Machinery | | 7,500 |
| Current Assets | | |
| Inventories | 7,250 | |
| Accounts Receivable | 4,385 | |
| Bank Balance | 4,320 | 15,955 |
| | | £23,455 |
| Total Assets | | |
| **CAPITAL & LIABILITIES** | | |
| Capital a/c | | |
| Opening Capital | 3,000 | |
| Profit in Year | 9,850 | |
| | 12,850 | |
| Drawings | (4,000) | |
| Closing Capital | | 8,850 |
| LOANS | | 6,750 |
| CURRENT LIABILITIES | | |
| Accounts Payable | 5,350 | |
| VAT due | 2,505 | |
| | | £7,855 |
| Total Capital & Liabilities | | £23,455 |

## Chapter 5

### A.1

|                           | Straight Line ( 6 years) | Reducing Balance 25% |
|---------------------------|-------------------------:|---------------------:|
| Cost                      | 24,000                   | 24,000               |
| Year 1 Depreciation *     | 3,000                    | 6,000                |
| Year 1 NBV                | 21,000                   | 18,000               |
| Year 2 Depreciation       | 3,000                    | 4,500                |
| Year 2 NBV                | 18,000                   | 13,500               |
| Year 3 Depreciation       | 3,000                    | 3,375                |
| Year 3 NBV                | 15,000                   | 10,125               |
| Year 4 Depreciation       | 3,000                    | 2,531                |
| Year 4 NBV                | 12,000                   | 7,594                |
| Year 5 Depreciation       | 3,000                    | 1,898                |
| Year 5 NBV                | 9,000                    | 5,695                |
| Year 6 Depreciation       | 3,000                    | 1,424                |
| Year 6 NBV                | 6,000                    | 4,271                |
| * note (24,000 - 6,000)/6 |                          |                      |

## Chapter 6

### A.1
Cash Book

|                          |       | Opening Balance      | 2,500 |
|--------------------------|------:|----------------------|------:|
| Cheques received         | 3,100 | Cheques paid out     | 6,250 |
| Balance Carried Forward  | 5,650 |                      |       |
| Totals                   | 8,750 | Totals               | 8,750 |
|                          |       | Balance Brought Down | 5,650 |

## A.2

### Sales Ledger

| | | | |
|---|---|---|---|
| Opening Balance | 2,700 | | |
| Invoiced Sales | 8,000 | Cheques received | 3,100 |
| | | Balance Carried Forward | 7,600 |
| Totals | 10,700 | Totals | 10,700 |
| Balance Brought Down | 7,600 | | |

## Chapter 7

### A.1

| | | |
|---|---|---|
| Operating Profit (PBIT) | £55,000 | |
| Interest Paid | 17,000 | |
| | £38,000 | |
| Taxation | 9,000 | |
| Profit after Tax | £29,000 | |
| | | |
| | | |
| Ordinary Shares | | 25,000 |
| Retained Profits (1.1.2014) | 10,000 | |
| Profit for y/e 31.12.14 | £29,000 | |
| Less Dividends Paid | 13,800 | |
| Retained Profits (31.12.2014) | | £25,200 |
| Equity Value | | 50,200 |

| A.2 | | |
|---|---|---|
| Share Capital | | £ |
| Ordinary Shares 400,000 shares of £0.40 | | 160,000 |
| Retained Profits to date | 240,000 | |
| Profit for year | 95,000 | |
| Dividends Paid | (15,000) | |
| Total Retained Profits at 31.12.2014 | | 320,000 |
| Equity Value | | £480,000 |

Therefore each share is now worth £480,000 ÷ 400,000 = £1.20

This shows a tripling of Share Value since Share Issue.

## Chapter 8

A.1

| RATIOS | Measure | Calculation | Previous Year |
|---|---|---|---|
| Profitability | | | |
| Return on Capital Employed (%) | % | 29% | 34 % |
| Return on Sales (%) | % | 13% | 18 % |
| Gross Margin (%) | % | 49% | 56 % |
| | | | |
| Financial Status | | | |
| Current | X:1 | 3.4 | 2.0 |
| Acid Test (Quick Ratio) | X:1 | 2.3 | 1.4 |
| Gearing (accountants) % | % | 56% | 48 % |
| | | | |
| Activity (Efficiency) Ratios | | | |
| Inventory Days | days | 91 | 110 |
| Accounts Receivable (Debtors) | days | 76 | 60 |
| Accounts Payable (Creditors) | days | 63 | 47 |

This shows an overall reducing profitability for Blaster Ltd. although still a good ROCE, a sound liquidity although reducing but an improving gearing coming down from a high level. Inventory days have fallen nicely. However, debtor days have worsened and suppliers may be withholding supplies to Blaster Ltd. as payment times have slipped.

A.2

| RATIOS | Measure | Calculation | Previous |
|---|---|---|---|
| Profitability | | | Year |
| Return on Capital Employed (%) | % | 71% | 71 % |
| Return on Sales (%) | % | 20% | 20 % |
| Gross Margin (%) | % | 61% | 61 % |
| | | | |
| Financial Status | | | |
| Current | X:1 | 2.3 | 2.3 |
| Acid Test (Quick Ratio) | X:1 | 1.1 | 1.1 |
| Gearing (accountants) % | % | 46% | 46 % |
| | | | |
| Activity (Efficiency) Ratios | | | |
| Inventory Days | days | 222 | 222 |
| Accounts Receivable (Debtors) | days | 76 | 76 |
| Accounts Payable (Creditors) | days | 30 | 30 |

This shows an overall steady profitability for Claxton Ltd. with a high ROCE, a sound steady liquidity with gearing steady but on the high side. Inventory days are again steady but very high. Debtor and Creditor days are steady but care must be taken in expanding as bills are paid over twice as quickly as money is collected.

## Chapter 9

A.1

**Sources:**

| | |
|---|---:|
| Profit | 75 |
| Add Depreciation | 50 |
| Adjusted Profit | 125 |
| Loan Increase | 70 |
| Decrease in Inventories | 135 |
| Change in Accounts Payable | 50 |
| Change in Accounts Receivable | 50 |
| Share Issue | 25 |
| (A) | 455 |

**Uses:**

| | |
|---|---:|
| Purchase of Fixed Assets (B) | 400 |
| Net Movement in Funds (A-B) | 55 |
| | |
| Movement in Bank (£200 to £255) | 55 |

A.2

Firstly, although making a profit, the cash flow from operating activities shows a negative of £16,000. This is primarily due to the poor management of the working capital. The money due in has increased (by £20,000) and the money due out has reduced substantially (by £35,000) and although there has been some minor improvement in the inventory management which has gone down by £4,000, this will put pressure on short term cash flow.

The cash flow from investing activities would look to have kept the company in reasonable shape as although there was a significant machinery purchase, there was a large income from the sale of a subsidiary company.

Cash flow from financing activities is again negative, caused by large loan repayments and dividend payments although there has been financing help from a share issue.

Overall, the cash has improved marginally (by £6,300) but there is still a substantial negative cash position (£43,400) and it would appear that the sale of the subsidiary company has been a lifesaver.

Chapter 11

A.1

| | Volume | Price | |
|---|---|---|---|
| Materials A | 30 | £2.50 | £75.00 |
| Materials B* | 20 | £3.00 | £60.00 |
| Total Material Costs | | | £135.00 |
| Labour | 15 | £12.00 | £180.00 |
| Prime Costs | | | £315.00 |
| Overheads | £75,000 ÷ 600 batches | | 125.00 |
| Total Cost per batch | | | £440.00 |
| Total cost per unit | £440 ÷ 12 =per batch | | £36.67 |

* Cost of the wastage should be included

| A.2 | Method | Totals | Manufacturing | Assembly |
|---|---|---|---|---|
| Manufacturing consumables | Direct | 4,000 | 4,000 | |
| Assembly consumables | Direct | 6,000 | | 6,000 |
| Supervisory wages | Staff Numbers | 45,000 | 9,000 | 36,000 |
| Canteen costs | Staff Nos | 18,000 | 3,600 | 14,400 |
| Rent Costs | Area | 30,000 | 10,000 | 20,000 |
| Machinery Maintenance | Machine Value | 12,000 | 8,000 | 4,000 |
| Heating & Lighting | Area | 18,000 | 6,000 | 12,000 |
| Total Overheads | | £133,000 | £40,600 | £92,400 |

A.2 Part 2

Manufacturing Overhead recovery rate = £40,600 ÷ 500 = £81.20/machine hour.

Assembly Overhead recovery rate = £92,400 ÷ 1,500 = £61.60/labour hour.

A.2 Part 3

| | |
|---|---|
| Material costs | £500.00 |
| Labour Costs (4 labour hours x £20/hour) | 80.00 |
| Prime Costs | 580.00 |
| Manufacturing Overheads (2 machine hrs x £81.20/machine hour) | £162.40 |
| Assembly Overheads (4 labour hrs x £61.60/labour hour) | 246.40 |
| Total Cost of product | £988.80 |

## A.3

| Volume | 2000 | 1500 | |
|---|---|---|---|
| | Teddy Bears | Dolls | Totals |
| Direct Costs | 14,000 | 6,000 | 20,000 |
| Overheads | £4,620 | £1,980 | £6,600 |
| Total Costs | 18,620 | 7,980 | 26,600 |
| | | | |
| Cost per product | £9.31 | £5.32 | |

i.e. overheads for Teddy bears are (£14,000 ÷ £20,000) x £6,600

## Chapter 12

### A.1

| Situation 1 | | | | |
|---|---|---|---|---|
| Selling Price per ticket | | 220 | | |
| Variable Costs (acc/food) | | 80 | | |
| Contribution per ticket | £ | 140.00 | | |
| | | | | |
| Fixed Costs | | | | |
| Rock groups | | 2,500,000 | | |
| Other Fixed costs | | 1,500,000 | | |
| Total Fixed Costs | £ | 4,000,000 | | |
| | | | | |
| Break-even (FC/Contrib/unit) | £ | 4,000,000 | 28,571 | Tickets |
| | £ | 140.00 | | |
| | | | | |
| Budgeted Sales of tickets | | 35,000 | | |
| | | | | |
| Margin of safety | =(35,000-28571) ÷ 35,000 | | 18.4% | |
| | | | | |
| Budgeted Profit | =140 x 35,000 - 4,000,000 | | £900,000 | |

| Situation 2 | | | | |
|---|---|---|---|---|
| Selling Price per ticket | | 100 | | |
| Variable Costs (acc/food) | | 10 | | |
| Contribution per ticket | £ | 90.00 | | |
| | | | | |
| Fixed Costs | | | | |
| Rock groups | | 2,000,000 | | |
| Other Fixed costs | | 1,500,000 | | |
| Total Fixed Costs | £ | 3,500,000 | | |
| | | | | |
| Break-even (FC/Contrib/unit) | £ | 3,500,000 | 38,889 | Tickets |
| | £ | 90.00 | | |
| | | | | |
| Budgeted Sales of tickets | | 50,000 | | |
| | | | | |
| Margin of safety | =(50,000-33,333) ÷ 50,000 | | 22.2% | |
| | | | | |
| Budgeted Profit | =90 x 50,000 - 3,500,000 | | £1,000,000 | |

Situation 2 would be the better proposition as it shows a higher budgeted profit, a lower commitment of fixed costs and a higher margin of safety. However, it would need to sell 10,318 more tickets to break-even (38,889 - 28,571) but these are at a much lower price but customers would need to supply their own accommodation, food etc.

## A.2

| | a) Profit | b) break-even |
|---|---|---|
| Units | 10 | 9 |
| | | |
| Sales | 40,000 | 36,000 |
| Variable Costs (40%) | 16,000 | 14,400 |
| Contribution | 24,000 | 21,600 |
| Fixed Costs | 21,600 | 21,600 |
| Profit | £2,400 | Nil |

| | b) max profit | c) |
|---|---|---|
| Units | 15 | 10 |
| | | |
| Sales | 60,000 | 40,000 |
| Variable Costs (40%) | 24,000 | 14,400 (36%) |
| Contribution | 36,000 | 25,600 |
| Fixed Costs | 21,600 | 21,600 |
| Profit | £14,400 | £4,000 |

## A.3

Firstly, the total costs should be broken down for each product and we quickly see that each product makes a contribution.

| A.3 | Totals | T-Shirts | Jumpers | Jeans |
|---|---|---|---|---|
| Sales | 90,000 | 51,000 | 21,000 | 18,000 |
| Variable Costs | 24,250 | 12,750 | 5,250 | 6,250 |
| Contribution | 65,750 | 38,250 | 15,750 | 11,750 |
| Fixed Costs | 49,500 | 25,500 | 10,500 | 13,500 |
| Profit | 16,250 | 12,750 | 5,250 | (1,750) |

If the jeans line was eliminated, not only would the contribution of £11,750 be lost but also it could affect the sales of the other products adversely. Secondly, if the Jeans were eliminated, how many of the fixed costs would vanish if any. Those left would need to be borne by the remaining products. After eliminating the £11,750 contribution, it would need to be replaced by the other products or a new product.

A.4

| A.4 | Shrieker | Ear Splitter | Nerve buster |
|---|---|---|---|
| Contribution/unit | £30 | £48 | £45 |
| Bells/unit | 3 | 4 | 5 |
| Contribution/bell | £10 | £12 | £9 |
| Priority | 2 | 1 | 3 |

| | Units | Bells | Contribution |
|---|---|---|---|
| Maximise Earsplitter | 2,000 | 8,000 | £96,000 |
| Ditto   Shrieker | 6,000 | 18,000 | 180,000 |
| Balance of bells on | | | |
| NerveBuster | 400 | 2,000 | 18,000 |
| Totals | | 28,000 | £294,000 |
| Less Fixed Costs | | | 250,000 |
| Net profit | | | £44,000 |

If we had prioritised on products with highest contribution per unit (which we do when there is no limiting factor) what would the result have been?

# A.5

a) Stage 1 - Calculate product marginal cost to establish the variable cost %

| | |
|---|---:|
| Material Cost | £1,000 |
| Labour 5 x £40 | 200 |
| Variable costs | 1,200 |
| Selling Price | £2,000 |
| Contribution | £800 |

Therefore contribution % is (800/2000) x 100 = 40% and variable costs are 60% of the sales.

Stage 2 - Calculate break-even turnover and so capacity (divide b/e by 40%) and so maximum profit.

| | B/E | Capacity |
|---|---:|---:|
| Units | 70 | 175 |
| Sales | 140,000 | 350,000 |
| Vary Costs (60%) | 84,000 | 210,000 |
| Contribution (40%) | 56,000 | 140,000 |
| Fixed Costs | 56,000 | 56,000 |
| Profit | Nil | 84,000 Max |

b) Capacity is 175 units. If each employee can produce 1/week for 35 weeks then there will be 175/35 = 5 employees needed.

c) Steps 1) increase fixed costs by £32,000. 2) Increase profit by 20,000. (20% of £100,000). 3) Work model backwards.

| | B/E | | Capacity | |
|---|---|---|---|---|
| Units | 70 | 175 | | 240 |
| Sales | 140,000 | 350,000 | | 480,000 |
| Vary Costs (60%) | 84,000 | 210,000 | | 288,000 |
| Contribution (40%) | 56,000 | 140,000 | | 192,000 (÷ 40%) |
| Fixed Costs | 56,000 | 56,000 | +32,000 | 88,000 |
| Profit | Nil | 84,000 | + 20,000 | 104,000 |

<u>They would therefore need to produce 65 extra units.</u>

d) Break-even chart. (See Appendix 5)

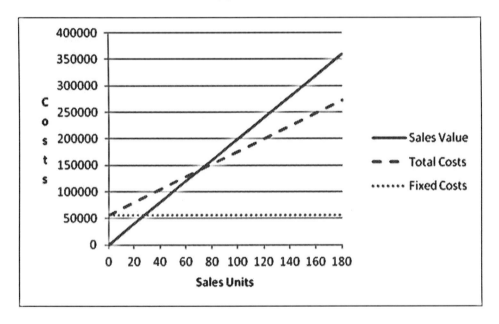

# Chapter 13

## A.1

|  | Budget | Actual | Variance |
|---|---|---|---|
|  | £ | £ | £ |
| Sales | 21,000 | 20,400 | (600) |
| Direct Materials | 8,400 | 9,000 | (600) |
| Direct Labour | 6,500 | 5,300 | 1,200 |
| Variable Overhead | 3,000 | 2,900 | 100 |
| Fixed Overhead | 2,200 | 2,400 | (200) |
| Profit | 900 | 800 | (100) |

Overall the profit has fallen short of budget by £100. This is explained by sales being under budget by £600, materials being over budget by £600 and fixed overheads also being over budget. The position was saved by a large favourable variance of £1,200 in the labour and a small one for variable overheads. The problem is that some of these costs are variable and as sales have fallen on budget, we would expect materials, labour and variable overheads to also fall.

## A.2

The units increase is 1,000 on 3,000 or 1/3$^{rd}$ and the materials has also risen by 1/3$^{rd}$ (£5,000/£15,000) so the materials are all variable.

The rent has not moved making it fixed.

The telephone has risen £1,500 (1/4) for an increase in units of 1,000 (1/3) making it a semi=variable cost.

Step 1 Increase in costs is £1,500 (£7,500 - £6,000), increase in activity is 1,000 units (4,000 – 3,000)

Step 2 This increase in costs must all be variable so calculate the variable cost/unit by dividing the increase in costs by the increase in units

i.e £1,500 ÷ 1,000 = £1.50/unit.

Step 3 Apply this variable cost rate to either activity level to work out the variable costs at that level. E.g 3,000 units @ £1.50/unit = £4,500

Step 4 Deduct the £4,500 from the total costs at that activity level to arrive at the fixed costs. E.g. £6,000 - £4,500 = £1,500 fixed costs.

The budget for 7,000 units would be as follows:

| Units | 3,000 | 4,000 | 7,000 |
|---|---|---|---|
| Materials | 15,000 | 20,000 | 35,000 |
| Rent | 7,000 | 7,000 | 7,000 |
| Telephone | 6,000 | 7,500 | 12,000 |

Materials directly variable, Rent fixed and telephone semi-variable.

Note telephone costs would be fixed cost £1,500 plus variable cost 7,000 units @ £1.50/unit = £12,000

A.3

| A3 | | Original Budget | y/e 31st March 2014 Flexed Budget | Actual | Variance |
|---|---|---|---|---|---|
| Number of Meals | | 36,000 | 43,200 | 43,200 | |
| | | | | | |
| *Expenditure* | | £ | £ | £ | £ |
| Provisions | | 64,800 | 77,760 | 74,300 | 3,460 |
| *Labour* | | | | | |
| - Supervisor | | 20,000 | 20,000 | 20,500 | -500 |
| - Staff | | 50,000 | 53,600 | 51,400 | 2,200 |
| Heat & Light | | 5,000 | 5,000 | 6,000 | -1,000 |
| Administration | | 8,600 | 9,320 | 10,100 | -780 |
| Total Exp. | | 148,400 | 165,680 | 162,300 | 3,380 |
| | | | | | |
| *Income* | £4.30 | 154,800 | 185,760 | 185,760 | 0 |
| | | | | | |
| *Surplus* | | 6,400 | 20,080 | 23,460 | 3,380 |

Notes

- To arrive at a flexed budget, the variable costs need to be adjusted for the increase in activity by multiplying by the new activity ÷ original budget activity or 43,200 ÷ 36,000 = 1.2
- Provisions are all directly variable at (or £1,80/meal) £64,800 × 1.20 = £77,760
- Supervisor is a fixed cost
- Variable costs of staff should be budgeted at £50,000 – Fixed Costs (4 × £8,000) = £18,000 or £0.50 per meal. Flexed budget

is therefore £32,000 + .50 x 43,200 = £53,600 (alternatively £32,000 + 1.2 x 18,000)

- Admin costs again should be re-budgeted with variable costs as (£8,600 - £5,000) = £3,600 x 1.2 = £4,320 plus fixed costs of £5,000 = £9,320.

The interpretation is now much more relevant:

- Provisions are now well under budget meaning good food cost management and portion control. The only worry is whether customers are leaving hungry!
- The supervisor has been paid extra on a fixed cost so this needs investigating.
- Again big savings on staff costs. Is this due to staff not receiving their rightful incentive payments of £0.50/meal or is the restaurant managing with less staff hours?
- Heat & light is a fixed cost and well over budget. Has fuel price increased or is there poor control with wastage? Would an economy drive help?
- Administration costs are still over budget but only just over half the original adverse variance. Cause needs investigating.
- Originally, overall the income was hiding the deficit on the expenses. With the new budget, this is not the case and in fact the overall expenditure budget has a favourable variance of £3,380.

# Chapter 14

## A.1

| Hole in the Dosh Ltd | | 6 months ended 30/6/0X | | | | | |
|---|---|---|---|---|---|---|---|
| | | | | | | | |
| Invoiced sales (note) | 28,000 | 28,000 | 28,000 | 40,000 | 40,000 | 40,000 | |
| **RECEIPTS** | *Jan* | *Feb* | *Mar* | *Apr* | *May* | *Jun* | *Total* |
| ACC Receivable | 12,000 | 36,000 | | | | | 48,000 |
| Cash Sales | 14,000 | 14,000 | 14,000 | 20,000 | 20,000 | 20,000 | 102,000 |
| Credit Sales | | | 14,000 | 14,000 | 14,000 | 20,000 | 62,000 |
| Gov Grant | | | | | 15,000 | | 15,000 |
| Total Receipts | 26,000 | 50,000 | 28,000 | 34,000 | 49,000 | 40,000 | 227,000 |
| **PAYMENTS** | | | | | | | |
| Acc Payable | 40,000 | | | | | | 40,000 |
| Purchases | | 7,000 | 7,000 | 7,000 | 10,000 | 10,000 | 41,000 |
| Wages | 10,000 | 10,000 | 10,000 | 12,000 | 12,000 | 12,000 | 66,000 |
| Overheads | 3,000 | 3,000 | 3,000 | 3,000 | 3,000 | 3,000 | 18,000 |
| Capital | | | 30,000 | | | | 30,000 |
| Total Payments | 53,000 | 20,000 | 50,000 | 22,000 | 25,000 | 25,000 | 195,000 |
| | | | | | | | |
| Cash Flow | (27,000) | 30,000 | (22,000) | 12,000 | 24,000 | 15,000 | 32,000 |
| | | | | | | | |
| Opening Bank | (40,000) | (67,000) | (37,000) | (59,000) | (47,000) | (23,000) | |
| Closing Bank | (67,000) | (37,000) | (59,000) | (47,000) | (23,000) | (8,000) | |

## Notes

- The opening bank is £20,000 overdrawn but allowing for the cheques to suppliers starts at £40,000.
- The invoiced sales are not part of the cash flow but there for 'note' purposes.
- Depreciation is ignored on cash flow as it is not a physical parting with money.

## Interpretation

- The overdraft limit of £55,000 is exceeded in January and March
- Two months show negative cash flow – January and March.
- The January cause is working capital (accounts payable) and these should be spread, stocks should be reduced (although this would not help January) and accounts receivable should be collected in quicker.
- The March problem is caused by the capital payment of £30,000. This is a long term asset and should be funded with long term finance. Perhaps a bank loan, share issue (although not really appropriate here, lease the equipment or just delay payment until the bank is into credit.

## Chapter 15

### A.1

| A.1 | Cash Flows | Cumulative |
|---|---|---|
| Year 0 | (30,000) | (30,000) |
| Year 1 | 10,000 | (20,000) |
| Year 2 | 12,000 | (8,000) |
| Year 3 | 6,000 | (2,000) |
| Year 4 | 4,000 | 2,000 |

Payback is 3 years plus 2,000 ÷ 4,000 × 12 months = 3 years 6 months (3.5 years)

A.2

ARR Calculations

Project 1

(sum of cash flows less capital) = £24,000

Average net cash flow per year (project life 5 years) = 24,000 ÷ 5 = £4,800

Average capital of 37,000 ÷ 2 = £18,500

Express Average Net Cash Flows as a % of Average Capital Employed

= 4,800 ÷ 18,500 × 100 = **25.9%**

Project 2

(sum of cash flows less capital) = £14,000

Average net cash flow per year (project life 4 years) = 14,000 ÷ 4 = £3,500

Average capital of 23,000 ÷ 2 = £11,500

Express Average Net Cash Flows as a % of Average Capital Employed

= 3,500 ÷ 11,500 × 100 = **30.4%**

So Project 2 would appear to be the best.

If Payback applied, Project 1 payback is 2.33 years and Project 2 payback is 3.07 years so Project 1 appears less risky due to a quicker payback.

## A.3

| A.3 | Project 1 | | 12% | | Project 2 | | |
|---|---|---|---|---|---|---|---|
| | Cash Flows | Factor | DCF | | Cash Flows | Factor | DCF |
| Year 0 | (37,000) | 1.000 | (37,000) | Year 0 | (23,000) | 1.000 | (23,000) |
| Year 1 | 14,000 | 0.893 | 12,500 | Year 1 | 3,000 | 0.893 | 2,679 |
| Year 2 | 19,000 | 0.797 | 15,147 | Year 2 | 7,000 | 0.797 | 5,580 |
| Year 3 | 12,000 | 0.712 | 8,541 | Year 3 | 12,000 | 0.712 | 8,541 |
| Year 4 | 10,000 | 0.636 | 6,355 | Year 4 | 15,000 | 0.636 | 9,533 |
| Year 5 | 6,000 | 0.567 | 3,405 | | | | |
| | | NPV | £8,948 | | | NPV | £3,333 |
| | | ARR | 25.9% | | | ARR | 30.4% |
| | | PB | 2.33 yrs | | | PB | 3.07 yrs |
| | | IRR | 23% | | | IRR | 17% |

This shows that the NPV for Project 1 is over double that of Project 2 because much of its cash flows are in the earlier years whereas project 2 cash flows are all later. The ARR would give the wrong decision unless over ruled by the payback result. The IRR would give project 1 the decision also being again 6% higher.

## A.4

| A | Capital | Cost | Weighted Cost |
|---|---|---|---|
| Equity | 150,000 | 14% | 21,000 |
| Loans | 50,000 | 5% | 2,500 |
| Totals | 200,000 | | 23,500 |
| | | | 11.8% |

| B | Capital | Cost | Weighted Cost |
|---|---|---|---|
| Equity | 40,000 | 18% | 7,200 |
| Loans | 80,000 | 8% | 6,400 |
| Totals | 120,000 | | 13,600 |
| | | | 11.3% |

Company A has the highest WACC at:**11.8%** (23,500 ÷ 200,000 x 100)

# 20. Glossary of Terms

- Absorption Costing – the establishment of the total cost of a product/service by adding the materials labour and overheads based on an overhead 'absorption' rate.
- Accounting Rate of Return (ARR) – a method of investment appraisal that relates the average profit made per year to the initial sum invested in a project.
- Accounting Standards – standards set by accounting standards boards to ensure comparability and fairness in the way accounts are presented.
- Activity Based Costing – a technique of separating costs into cost pools (rather than departments) so that a more accurate cost of a product/service can be established by allocating costs to a product by the product's demand for that resource.
- Activity Ratios – Ratios that describe the speed of turnover such as Inventory, Receivables and Payables. Sometimes called Efficiency Ratios.
- Amortisation – this is depreciation applied to an Intangible asset.
- Balance sheet – also called a Statement of Financial Position (SOFP), it is a summary of assets and liabilities of an organisation at one point in time. One of the three main year-end accounting statements.
- Break even – the point where sales equals total costs
- Budget – a plan of action expressed in financial terms usually for the ensuing 12 months
- Capital Investment appraisal – this describes a group of techniques used to asses and compare differing capital projects
- Capital Reserves – a reserve not created through revenue trading but normally by the revaluation (usually upwards) of Non-Current assets

- Cash flow forecast – part of the budgetary control procedures, this is a management accounting statement that summarises other budgets (sales, purchases, overheads, labour, capital) into the predicted effects on the bank balance. It is often confused with the cash flow statement which is a historical statement of what has happened to the cash in the past.
- Cost of Sales – the direct costs deducted from sales before arriving at the gross profit
- Cost Plus Pricing – the total cost of a product or service plus a markup to cover profit
- Costing for Decision making – the breakdown of costs between fixed and variable costs for the purpose of making decisions such as break even analysis and product line decisions
- Current Assets – Short term assets used in the trading cycle such as cash, Accounts Receivable and Inventories
- Current Liabilities – liabilities due within 12 months such as accounts payable and overdraft
- Debenture – A loan secured on the assets of a company through a Debenture Trust Deed. It may be through a bank or there could be a whole mix of 'Debenture Holders' if the company sold these Loan Notes on the stockmarket.
- Depreciation – the amount by which a Non-Current asset is written down during a year.
- Discounted Cash Flow (DCF) – using the time value of money to bring future costs and incomes back to today values.
- EBITDA – Earnings before Interest, tax, depreciation and amortisation. Used as a comparative measure where the level of depreciation and amortisation in some industries can have a distorting effect on comparisons.

- Financial Status Ratios – Ratios that describe the stability of a company such as gearing and interest cover in the long term and Current ratio and Acid test in the short term
- Fixed Assets – the former name of the Non-Current assets section in the Balance Sheet
- Fixed Budget – a budget that assumes one level of activity and restricts spending on all cost centres to a 'fixed' level.
- Flexible Budgeting – a budget that allows movement in the variable costs of a budget statement related to the changes in activity (eg sales).
- Gearing – the level of debt expressed as a percentage of its total long term finances. High gearing means high borrowing.
- Gross Profit – sales less cost of sales
- Income Statement - Formerly known as the profit & loss account it shows the sales less the running costs and hence the profit of an organisation over a period. One of the three main year-end accounting statements.
- Incremental Budget – a budget based on the previous year and adjusted for inflation and other known differences
- Insolvent – where a company's assets are less than its liabilities (negative net assets)
- Intangible Assets – Those Non-Current assets that are not 'touchable' such as patents, brand values and goodwill.
- Internal Rate of Return (IRR) – this gives an annualised compounded percentage return on a project
- Investor Ratios – ratios used by investors to assess their investment such as Earnings per Share, P/E ratio, dividend cover and yield
- Ledger – a book of account

- Liquidity – the ability of an organisation to meet its short term debts on time. It often refers to having adequate short term cash resources.
- Marginal Cost – the cost of making one more item i.e. the variable costs
- Marginal Pricing – pricing a product or service above the variable costs to achieve a contribution
- Net Present Value (NPV) – this gives the absolute return over the life of a project after allowing for the time value of money
- Net Profit – sales less costs. Profit may be before or after Interest, tax or depreciation
- Non-Current Assets – Assets that are not purchased with the intention of selling in the short term such as buildings and machinery. They remain in the Balance Sheet at the year-end as they are not fully consumed.
- Non-Current Liabilities – liabilities payable over more than 12 months such as loans
- Operating Profit – the same as Profit Before Interest and Tax (PBIT) or Earnings before Interest and Tax (EBIT).
- Ordinary Shares – the shares (and shareholders) that control a company and have the highest risk and return
- Payback – a technique of investment appraisal that establishes the time it takes to recover the capital costs of a project
- PBIT – profit before interest and tax. The same as EBIT (Earnings before Interest and tax) and Operating Profit
- Preference Shares – shares that are somewhere between Ordinary Shares and loans usually with a fixed rate of dividend and little controlling interest
- Profit & Loss account – the former name of the Income Statement

- Profitability Ratios – ratios that measure profitability such as return on sales, gross profit and return on capital
- Reserves – the sum of all the company reserves such as retained profits plus the capital reserves
- Retained Profit – profit after all deductions and after dividends paid to shareholders
- Revenue Reserves – all the Retained Profits in a company since its commencement
- Sales – the amount invoiced to customers during the year. Also called revenue, income or turnover.
- Shareholders' Equity – the Balance Sheet value of a company expressed as the Ordinary Shares plus the Reserves.
- Solvency – the ability of a company to meet its debts
- Stakeholder – anyone with an interest in an organisation's activities. Can be Primary (contractual) or Secondary.
- Statement of Cash Flows – or cash flow statement this shows how an organisation's profit has been converted into cash at the year-end after allowing for capital expenditure and finance raising activities.  One of the three main year-end accounting statements.
- Statement of Financial Position (SOFP) – Another term for Balance Sheet
- Variance Analysis – the analysis of the differences between the budget and the actual results
- Working Capital – defined as current assets less current liabilities
- Zero Based Budget (ZBB) – where a budget for a department is drawn up assuming the 'department' is being set up from nothing to do its required tasks. It does not rely on what resources were used in the past.

# 21. Further Recommended Reading

- Atrill & McLaney, *Accounting and Finance for Non-specialists* (7th Edition, 2010).
- Atrill, Peter, *Financial Management for Decision Makers* (6th Edition, 2011).
- Drury, Colin, *Cost and Management Accounting: An Introduction* (7th Revised
- Edition, 2011).
- France, Richard *Finance for Purchasing Managers* (2013) (specifically for those in purchasing)
- Mary Carey, Cathy Knowles, Jane Towers-Clark, *Accounting – a smart approach*
- Millichamp, A.H., *Finance for Non-financial Managers: An Active-learning Approach* (3rd Edition, 2000).

# ABOUT THE AUTHOR

Richard France is a Chartered Accountant (FCA) and has an MBA from Henley Business School. Having qualified, he became a Finance Director of a 300 employee manufacturing business followed by a 20 year period combining lecturing at University with financial consultancy and training work in his own company. Prior to his current full-time role lecturing in Finance and Accounting at Manchester Metropolitan University, he spent several years working for PMMS Consulting Group which is an International niche consultancy company specialising in Purchasing Training and Consultancy. He has worked with many well-known public companies in retail, services and manufacturing.